the

secrets

of

self-employment

THIS IS A CARLTON BOOK

Text copyright © 2001 Mongrel Worlds Limited
Design copyright © 2001 Carlton Books

This edition published by Carlton Books Limited 2001
20 Mortimer Street, London W1T 3JW

A CIP catalogue for this book is available from the British Library.

ISBN 1 84222 370 4

Project Editor: Vanessa Daubney
Art Director: Mark Lloyd
Editorial and Design: Terry Burrows/The Orgone Company
Production Manager: Sarah Corteel

Printed in Italy

the secrets

of

self-employment

terry burrows

CARLTON
BOOKS

contents

foreword

by alvin hall

I always like to say that self-employment chose me rather than my choosing it. I was working for a large corporation when Powers That Be decided to downsize the division for which I worked. I have to admit that I was not emotionally devastated by this experience, as some of my colleagues were. Instead, I was just mad!

AS I WALKED OUT OF the building for the last time, I felt as if I were in a dream sequence from a 1940's movie. The following phrases kept echoing alternately in my mind: "Success is the best revenge" and "As God as my witness, I'll never…" (you know the rest of the line.) I was channelling my rage, my fist filled with the crumpled papers of my redundancy and raised above toward the heavens in willful determination to survive – and succeed.

When I started, these adages became my mantra, my motivation, indeed my *raison d'etre*.

Becoming self-employed is like taking a great leap of faith – in yourself

But eventually this raw motivation came into contact with the reality of being a self-employed person. Becoming self-employed is like taking a great leap of faith – in yourself. Internally, you wonder if you will be able to corral your assets and experiences, while at the same time overcoming your weaknesses and controlling your demons. Externally, there's an endless series of questions about just running a business: What is the best legal structure for my business? What kinds of insurance do I need? What kind of book keeping system is best for my type of business?

How do I handle the tax returns? This endless stream of questions always lead (sometimes in exasperation or at other times in desperation) to one final question: "Are there any people, services or agencies that can give me guidance in this new world of self-employment?"

I went to bookstores to find answers to these external questions. There I found that most of the books on self-employment were too theoretical. I wanted a guide, like this book, that would: 1) provide information in clear, easily understood language; and 2) help me to make myself smarter about key decisions and issues that would affect my business immediately and over the long term.

This book, *The Secrets of Self-Employment* will definitely shorten your learning curve for the practical aspects of getting your business up and running. It makes you aware of decisions you'll have to make as the business grows, thus giving you time to think and plan for them, instead of just reacting when they occur. It offers solutions to problems that every self-employed person encounters. The totality of the how-to advice, the business roadmap, and the insights in this book will give you that much needed first leg-up toward becoming a successful self-employed person.

Anyone who has been self-employed will tell you that during the first few years, it is business that controls your life

But the information in this book is only part of the total equation. Experience will also be your teacher. My self-employed friends and I believe there are three important insights that all of us had separately in the first few years of business. In our separate business worlds, each of us thought we were having a unique experience. We now laugh about our somewhat delusional, undoubtedly egocentric desire to feel "special". I want to share these simple insights here because I am convinced that keeping them in mind as key reference points early in your decision-making process will help you in two ways. First, it will help you to avoid some of the pitfalls that can quickly leave your dreams unfulfilled. And second, they help keep your eyes on the prize that you're really trying to achieve: becoming and remaining a successful self-employed person.

INSIGHT #1: FOCUS ON THE BUSINESS, NOT THE LIFESTYLE

While writing this foreword, I got a call from a woman who had recently started a private legal practice. I was thrilled for her. But my joy turned to concern when she made the following statement: "I'm looking forward to being able to live the way I want and being in control of my life." This is certainly the dream of all of us who are self-employed. But this statement told me that this woman was starting her business for the right reason, but with the wrong focus. This reflects what I call the "*feel good before you do good*" mentality. This can cause you to start living in the style of your rosy future before you have actually achieved or earned it.

As a self-employed person, your efforts must stay tightly focused on getting your business up and running successfully. Do not focus on the lifestyle you hope it will eventually yield. Anyone who has been self-employed will tell you that during the first few years, it is business that controls your life. Your life will not control the business. You will work harder – and with greater productivity and satisfaction – during this time than you ever did when you worked for someone else. Expect this period of working day and night and night and day to last between two and five years. That's right! Success rarely comes overnight for a self-employed person. You have to stick with the three "Ps": patience, productivity, and persistence. And you have to apply them to yourself, as at the same time you are being the CEO, bookkeeper, marketeer, shipper, administrative assistant, cook, maid. And, who knows, you may even give birth to a baby or two.

INSIGHT #2: YOUR CLIENTS ARE YOUR BOSSES

How many of us have said that one of the reasons we want to work for ourselves is that we will no longer have any bosses? Indeed, self-employment does mean that you are not subject to the caprice, whim, and eccentricities of one person. Instead, you may be subject to the caprice, whim, and eccentricities of many people – your clients.

In the early days of self-employment, you have to take whatever business comes along to keep your enterprise going. This often means dealing with people you may fundamentally dislike, or whose habits may drive you crazy. I have a client who tells me everything in triplicate. When he feels there is something important to say, he leaves messages on my office phone, my home phone, and, then calls my office phone reconfirm the message and to express his desire to have my mobile phone number. Well, he ain't going to get

it – ever! In the early days of my business, this behaviour use to make me so crazy that I would be exasperated after listening to the messages that I would have to lie down. I'd find myself having imaginary conversations with him about how to correct this behaviour.

Then one day the message of this situation dawned on me: I had to learn to manage myself better relative to this client and every other client. I realised that this was the way he functioned and that I could not take it personally. And that as a self-employed person, I was only subjected to this a couple of hours each week. After all, I did not work for him full-time – thankfully!

Like it or not, as a self-employed person you still have bosses

Like or not, as a self-employed person you still have bosses. And in the early days when you are trying to build the business and are feeling most vulnerable, these clients can be demanding and unsympathetic. Keep in mind, however, that you are only dealing with them for a short time each day. Compartmentalise the experience so that it doesn't affect your other work. And remember that they are unlikely to change, so you have to make the adjustments in the way you deal with them. With the client described above, I simply no longer listen to the second and third messages. And I can't describe to you the private satisfaction I get from pushing the erase button on my answer phone.

INSIGHT #3: BE OBJECTIVE ABOUT YOUR BUSINESS – AND YOURSELF

I have done three shows about people who were starting or had started their own businesses. One of the young men from one program sent me an e-mail saying when he watched the show about the other entrepreneurs, he identified with their feeling that I was "coming to take their dream away". He then acknowledged the fact that those seemingly dream-destroying questions I asked made him think about his own situation. Asking yourself the hard questions and answering them cold-bloodedly is part of a reality check necessary to have you see the viability of your self-employment dream. If you can't see your business with any degree of detachment, then to me this is a warning sign. As I have seen over and over again, the emotion that prevents you from making yourself answer the difficult questions will surely cloud and distort your vision during the difficult times that all businesses experience.

> **Asking yourself the hard questions and then answering them cold-bloodedly is part of a reality check necessary to have you see the viability of your dream**

Applying your ability to evaluate your business objectively to yourself is also essential for long-term business success. And it is also one of the unexpected outcomes of being self-employed. Now, I don't mean that you have to share this self-knowledge information with everyone. After all, you do have your business image to worry about. But you must constantly assess yourself in order to inspire yourself, to improve yourself.

I do this by having conservations with myself while taking a bath or while in front of the mirror as I shave each morning. I chastise myself for repeating a habit that was not good for my business. I also talk about an accomplishment that was better than I expected. (Perhaps this is a sign of multiple personalities.) And I don't pat myself on the back for just doing my job well. That's what my clients expect. It's the exceptional problems or achievement that you want to correct or reinforce.

There are great joys and frustrations involved in being self-employed – especially in the early days. The joys will far out-weight the frustrations. And many of these specific frustrations will fade from memory, leaving you with only the wisdom of the experience. Self-employment is like sex, really. You're eager and nervous at first, and you make a few regrettable mistakes. And then more you do it, the better (hopefully) you will get at it. I look back on how naïve and inexperienced I was when I started my business over 10 years ago. A book such as this one – and some awareness of the three bits of wisdom above – would have been a godsend! Now that you have them, use them to thoughtfully guide your first steps into self-employment and to build your long-term success.

May the Force be with you!

Alvin Hall
July, 2001

manifestos

"The thing I lose patience with the most is the clock. Its hands move too fast. Time is really the only capital that any human being has, and the one thing that he can't afford to lose."

Thomas Alva Edison (1847-1931)

"Far away there in the sunshine are my highest aspirations. I may not reach them, but I can look up and see their beauty, believe in them, and try to follow them."

Louisa May Alcott (1832-1988)

"It's kind of fun to do the impossible."

Walt Disney (1901-1966)

"Chance favours only the prepared mind."

Louis Pasteur (1822-1895)

"If you want to make an apple pie from scratch, you must first create the universe."

Professor Carl Sagan (1934-1996)

"Obstacles are those frightful things you see when you take your eyes off your goal."

Henry Ford (1863-1947)

"While we are postponing, life speeds by."

Seneca (3BC-65AD)

"Don't dream it – *be it*."

Richard O'Brien (born 1942), The Rocky Horror Show

first
steps

1

in this chapter...

the quiet revolution

"The power of networks, the liberation offered by elect."

Stuart Crainer and Des Dearlove in *Generation Entrepreneur*

EXISTING NOTIONS OF what it means to "work for a living" are under siege. More and more of us are casting aside the shackles of our former corporate lives and striking out alone.

At the moment there are around 1.6 million self-employed professionals working in Great Britain. They represent something like 6% of the working population and contribute an estimated £65 billion to the UK economy. Projections from Foresight Research suggest that by the end of the decade, this number will have risen to 3.2 million. All of which this is beginning to have a profound impact on the traditional relationship between employer and employee.

Why should this be? It begins with the death of the "corporate promise". Since the late 1980s it has become increasingly clear that large companies – indeed, employers in general – can no longer be relied upon to provide the same levels of security that our parents' generation came to expect without question. In other words the days of having a "job for life" are gone forever. So why on earth should we want to bust a gut for the benefit of a distant, unknown group of

Employers can no longer be relied upon to provide the same levels of security that our parents' generation could expect

shareholders when experience tells us that the first sign of a dip in the market could just as easily end with a P45 and redundancy cheque?

Why, indeed. Consequently, as a working population, we are increasingly turning our backs on corporate life. More of us are understanding that there are clear benefits to self-reliance. We are more productive. We are more easily able to innovate. And — on the whole — we are wealthier as a result.

Knowledge workers are opening their eyes to the fact that the balance of power between company and worker is shifting in their favour

What's more, self-employment offers us the chance to live our lives in the way we choose. Indeed, for many of us, it's as much a lifestyle issue as an economic one. You can think of it as a statement of independence… of defiance, even.

With a continuing shift towards a knowledge-based economy, those with the relevant skills are opening their eyes to the fact that the balance of power between company and worker is shifting in their favour. The tables are being turned. They realise that *they* may be worth more to a carefully targeted client base than any single company could ever be to them. As Stuart Crainer and Des Dearlove point out in *Generation Entrepreneur*: "For a growing number of people, it's a no-brainer. Why, after all, would they want to line someone else's pockets? Why would they trust their skills to someone else? Why take that chance."

Welcome to the world of **Me UnLtd**.

WHAT'S SO GREAT ABOUT SELF-EMPLOYMENT?

To answer that one, let's look at the views of some of the people who are already doing it.

In 2000, Alodis, the service for self-employed professionals, commissioned pollsters MORI to perform the first ever in-depth study into Britain's self-employed. The result was the report *I Want To Be My Own Boss — Inside The New Self-Employed Revolution*. Let's look at the poll's key findings — they may provide you with some inspiration.

IS SELF-EMPLOYMENT MORE ENJOYABLE THAN HAVING A PERMANENT JOB?

86% said that is was.

There are many reasons for discarding a salaried position. For some it had always been a dream; for others who made and enjoyed the transition, it was redundancy that provided the impetus.

WHAT ARE THE WORST ASPECTS OF PERMANENT EMPLOYMENT?

70% said office politics.

For many others it was just a general dissatisfaction with office life: a dislike of employer, colleagues or the corporate culture. Other major gripes included unreasonable hours and poor management.

ARE THE SELF-EMPLOYED HAPPY?

78% said their quality of life had risen since leaving permanent employment.

This is perhaps the most significant point of all. The poll reinforces the common sense view that marching to your own drum-beat is likely to make for a more satisfying way of life. A common problem for those in permanent jobs is one of conflicting goals: the aims of employer and employee are simply not always well aligned. This traditional co-dependence has always relied on the idea of work being the simple purchase of labour in exchange for cash. But this age-old edifice begins to wobble when money ceases to be the driving factor.

One of the key attractions can be found in the fact that 88% of those polled claimed that being self-employed was far less about financial reward and more about quality of life. One area of particular note was the work/life balance, where 65% felt that they now had more

> **A common problem for those with permanent jobs is that company goal and employee goals are not necessarily the same**

TOO GOOD TO BE TRUE?

OK, we admit it. We've already bought into the idea of independence, and for many of us there could be no going back. But the Alodis/MORI poll did identify some areas of dissatisfaction.

The government came under heavy fire. It's quite clear that irrespective of which political party gets power, successive governments have seemed unable to get a handle on self-employment issues. The growth of the small business sector seems to be encouraged, and yet few benefits or breaks are on offer. Certainly a majority of those polled felt that the tax system as it relates to the self-employed could be somewhat fairer. Support from official government bodies was also thought be very poor, with over three-quarters claiming to have received receiving no help whatsoever during the crucial start-up phase. A particular bug-bear was bureaucracy, with 61% feeling strongly that the government was not doing enough to reduce regulations and "red-tape" for the self-employed.

Worse still, 80% of those polled believed that the late-payments legislation introduced in 1998 – giving small businesses the legal right to charge interest on outstanding debts – had almost no impact. Most of them felt it had not made their cash flow any more predictable, and few would claim that they would ever consider charging interest for fear of upsetting the relationship with their client.

Banks and financial institutions fared little better. 69% said that they had received little or no support from banks when starting up; 27% felt that these institutions had not been supportive through times of crisis, with almost half claiming that no support was offered when their business ran into financial difficulties; 17% felt that lack of support continued once they were up and running. A third also found trying to arrange a mortgage to be problematic.

There is no doubt that the self-employed way of life is not all roses.

time to do the things they enjoyed. Much of this can be attributed to the flexibility in working hours that comes with the territory. If you've been commissioned by a client to write a report, you can work on it between midnight and 6am, and then sleep through until the following afternoon if that's the way that suits you best. It makes no difference to your client.

ARE THE SELF-EMPLOYED MORE EFFECTIVE IN THEIR WORK?

72% felt they had become more entrepreneurial since leaving permanent work.

The vast majority of self-employed workers feel that they are considerably more productive and motivated than their "permie" counterparts. But there was an awareness that their freedom came at a price, 64% reporting that they now had to be more disciplined in their use of time.

One important side effect of this process is that 66% believed that they had grown in confidence as a result of the transition. This in turn enabled them to take on more demanding challenges than they would previously have done. It also makes procurement of future work easier.

WOULD THEY DO IT AGAIN?

85% said that with the benefit of hindsight they would STILL opt for self-employment.

This is a ringing endorsement: although it may take hard work and discipline, few regret making that transition. ●

POLL SUMMARY

90% are fairly or very satisfied with being self-employed

86% feel that working for themselves is more enjoyable than being employed

85% would take the same decision again to work for themselves

78% feel they now have a much better quality of life

72% think they have become more entrepreneurial

70% think that a lack of office politics is the best thing about self-employment

66% say they now have more time to think

66% feel they have become more confident

65% claim to have more time to do the things they enjoy

Source: Alodis/MORI poll, 2000

is self-employment for you?

For the self-employed, the difference between success and failure depends on one single asset: YOU. For some of us, that fact is simultaneously the most exciting AND scary aspect of the whole business. Before taking such a giant leap in personal responsibility, a bit of honest soul-searching is needed.

MAKE NO MISTAKE, the move from permanent employment to taking complete responsibility for you own working life will mean major upheaval. Not only will it take a lot of hard graft but it's also likely to create a considerable change to your lifestyle. To be brutally frank, if you're someone who places particular value on a secure or comfortable existence (whatever that might mean in an age where old-fashioned notions of "job security" are rapidly vanishing), you may not be naturally well suited to self-employment.

THAT'S NOT TO SAY THAT YOU CAN'T OR SHOULDN'T DO IT, THOUGH. It *does* mean that you'll need to become very aware of how your attitudes or aspects of your personality can work for and against you in the future. Most self-employed workers rely to a greater or lesser extent on the idea of "selling themselves" to potential clients for their business. And yet many of them – and you may be surprised at how many – for one reason or another find this

Looking for a comfortable, secure, stress-free existence? Self-employment may not be the right choice for you at the moment

> ❝ There is far more pressure now than there was before – for a start you're worry about missing out on work, even when there is plenty around. Not having to commute is a godsend, but I do miss the office banter, and being paid on time. ❞
>
> **Tom Downs, *journalist***

THE SECRETS OF SELF-EMPLOYMENT #1

Be honest with yourself: find out your weaknesses and consider how they can become positive traits

process in some way terrifying or demeaning. It has to be done, though, otherwise they don't make a living.

Relax, all we're saying here is that an awareness of problem areas up makes them easier to face (or circumvent) in the future. You're dealing with dreams here – don't let a negative attitude derail you before you get started.

THE RIGHT MINDSET

Nobody can easily predict how successful a shift from permanent work to self-employment will be. But there are a number of critical factors that will have a major bearing on the outcome. It's all about getting yourself into the right mindset. Let's take a look at your own attitudes as they stand today. How would you describe yourself? Are you self-motivated or are you happier being instructed by others? Are you self-disciplined? Do you enjoy the responsibility or satisfaction of

making life-altering decisions? Over the next few pages we'll look at some critically important areas that you will need to address.

DEDICATION

Here's a key word: DEDICATION. You might not have a boss checking up that you're working your contracted hours, but as a self-employed worker you'll almost certain to be eating into your spare time when you first start.

What's more, you'll do this voluntarily. And you won't feel that bad about it. Well, that may be pushing it a bit, but there's a good chance that you'll be squeezing the work of two people into an average working day – that requires both drive and energy. Going it alone is not for the slacker.

FLEXIBILITY

It doesn't necessarily matter what the product or service you are intending to sell might be, when you're self-employed you will have to get used to being something of a jack-of-all-trades. If you're a natural "dabbler", you may well really enjoy this aspect of your new life. ➡

GREAT MYTHS EXPLODED

WHEN YOU'RE SELF-EMPLOYED YOU CAN WORK AS FEW OR MANY HOURS AS YOU WANT. THINK AGAIN. While theoretically this may be true, research suggests the vast majority of self-employed professionals will find themselves working significantly LONGER hours. Indeed, it's estimated that on average they are likely to work 20% more than their "permie" counterparts.

Life is rarely dull when you're self-employed. You'll assemble a rare selection of skills – even if you didn't want some of them.

Whatever happens, though, whether you like it or not, you're going to have to develop skills as a salesman, marketeer, computer expert, office administrator, accountant, solicitor... and someone has to keep the place clean.

Your initial success is more likely to be governed by the way you deal with the things you DON'T do that well

were already self-employed. Break this theoretical day down into a series of tasks – no matter how mundane they might seem. These are all things that MUST be done if your business is to run smoothly. Now look at that list and ask yourself which of those tasks you would do well and those which would have you struggling. Be honest about this.

Here's an exercise for you to try out. Imagine, if you can, your day-to-day working life if you

In truth, the success of your first year in business is more likely to be governed by the way you deal with the things you DON'T do well.

> ❝ During my first month in my first "solo" office, I must've managed less than 20 hours doing anything remotely connected to law. The rest of the time I was juggling a ridiculous variety of unexpected jobs, from plumber and painter to cleaner and receptionist. It was a bit of a shock to the system. ❞
> **Helen Knights, *solicitor***

Take information technology, for example. It's more than likely that most of your business administration will be done using a computer. If right now you are barely able to find the on-off switch, then you will be in for some trying times. So think seriously about acquiring the necessary skills beforehand — at least if you don't want to find yourself wasting half a day trying to figure out how to print out an invoice.

COPING WITH STRESS

There's no getting away from it, leaving full-time employment can be a stressful thing to do. All of a sudden there are these new dimensions to your life that you've never had to worry about before. Things are different because, to all intents and purposes, now you *are* the business. With that in mind, ask yourself how you would react if:

- **A big order suddenly fell through**
- **You had so much work that you knew it could only be fulfilled by working round the clock**
- **Your running costs started to outweigh your income**
- **Your bank manager called in on a loan you couldn't afford to pay**
- **Sudden incapacity lost you a couple of weeks work**
- **You experienced a break-in in which your computer containing the only copies of your accounts was stolen**
- **A client threatened a lawsuit for something you did in the course of your work.**

Stress has a bad reputation, but without it not much work would ever get done. The key is in learning to stop it getting out of control — when it does that it's both bad for your health and for your working capacity.

FAMILY MATTERS

Your new working life is certain to affect both your family and social life. Getting a new venture off the ground will be stressful, requiring hard work and focussed attention. This can place considerable strain on your personal relationships. While you're likely to want, or even need, the support of those close to you, there will be times when it will be all too easy for them to feel ignored.

Although creating and keeping to a set of working hours is always highly recommended, there will be times — especially when you are getting started — that you will need to work those extra weekends and evenings. And taking family holidays may become extremely difficult. How will that affect the dynamics of your family?

It's clearly only right and proper that you should discuss such implications with those around you. That way they should at least be prepared for what might happen in the future. Here are some questions to ask yourself:

- How closely have you discussed your thoughts and ambitions with your partner?
- How do your family feel about the idea of you working at home?
- Are they willing to help out if necessary?
- Do they understand the financial implications?
- Are they prepared to accept a lower standard of living if necessary?
- Is your partner prepared (or able) to support you during the start-up phase?

Failing to resolve conflicts between the demands of work and the family is a famous strain on any relationship. But without your loved ones behind you, you're *guaranteed* a long, lonely ride.

Even the most thick-skinned individual would find any of the those previous scenarios worrying. But they *are* nonetheless the kinds of problems that many small businesses have to face. In order for you to succeed you need to be able to deal with them in a calm and clear-minded way.

FEAR OF FAILURE

When you start up on your own it can – and should – feel as if you are personally putting yourself on the line. Any success you enjoy should fill you with a great sense of pride and fulfilment, breeding the confidence that builds even more success. But what would happen if you experience a setback? Would it be a devastating personal tragedy? Or would you learn from the experience and simply move on?

Your business will not always run smoothly, that much can be guaranteed. You will encounter so many unfamiliar situations – especially at the beginning – that it would take a superhuman to avoid making at least some mistakes. Ultimately, the most successful entrepreneurs are the ones

> **❝** Failure is just a part of the culture of innovation. Accept it and become stronger. **❞**
> **Albert Yu, *senior vice-president, Intel***

> **❝** I've rewarded failures by giving out awards to people when they've failed, because they took a swing. **❞**
> **Jack Welch, *president, GE***

who can keep their egos under control and accept that errors are a natural part of learning. There's only one way that you can be completely certain you won't ever experience failure, and that's by not attempting anything in the first place.

There's only one way you can guarantee that you won't experience failure, and that's by not attempting anything in the first place

You may be surprised by how many of the most famous names in the world of business have failed ventures or even bankruptcies behind them. These figures have been able to assess and accept their situations and say to themselves: "OK, that's taught me a valuable lesson in how NOT to do it. Time to move on."

ISOLATION

One aspect of going it alone that can come as something of a surprise is the degree to which former work colleagues are missed. But that shouldn't seem so strange, really – most people, after all, spend as many of their waking hours at work as they do with their families. This inevitably creates powerful bonds. When these

> **❝** The first few weeks were great. I'd wake up every morning with such incredible motivation. But soon it began to dawn on me that I was actually missing the social interaction and buzz of my old office... very ironic in that the hostile atmosphere and lack of close colleagues had been a big factor in my leaving. **❞**
> **Joyce Alvarez, *journalist***

are taken away they can leave you feeling surprising lonely. But even if you can't currently stand to be in the same room as your co-workers, don't be surprised if you miss simply being surrounded by "real" people. Going solo can mean a shift from eight hours of human interaction to eight hours of isolation. Not everyone is well equipped to deal with that.

Self-employment can mean a shift from eight hours of interaction to eight hours of isolation – not everyone is equipped to deal with that

FINANCIAL SECURITY

For most of us, money is a major factor in our lives. It doesn't matter where we place it in our priorities, most of us need to keep earning in order to live. The obvious advantage of permanent employment is that it we can project within a little our income over the short and medium terms. This enables us to make reasonably accurate financial plans – if we want to buy something on a credit card and pay for over the next six months that's easy if you know what your income will be in six months time. Unless you're a contractor or "permalancer", self-employment will require a complete overhaul of the way you view money. During the course of a year your income will peak and trough making planning more difficult. You will be forced to make allowances for this.

STATUS

For many, success is defined by the position they hold within a company. The chain of command from chairman down to trainee is unequivocal. For the self-employed, that hierarchy simply does not exist. Even if your income increases ten-fold, your "status" will no longer be at all clear. As the term itself implies, self-employment is a self-centred lifestyle. From now on you are only in competition with yourself. Your success can only truly be measured in terms of the goals you have chosen.

REALITY

You have a better chance of making a success of being self-employed if your feet are firmly anchored in reality. We know that something like a third of all new businesses are no longer active within three years of set-up. But you can bet that a significant proportion of that failure rate is made up from the "fingers-crossed" brigade. These are the businesses that are founded on hope above any realistic assessment.

Those most likely to succeed are able to calmly review their abilities and ambitions and admit to themselves: "I know where I want to go; I know how to get there; but I realise that first I need to be able to do X, Y, Z – then I'll be on target."

TOTAL COMMITMENT

If you have one hundred per cent faith in what you are doing you can overcome all odds, succeeding over seemingly better equipped, trained or qualified competitors. But let's be brutal about this: IF YOU GO INTO A NEW VENTURE HALF-HEARTEDLY, YOU <u>WILL</u> FAIL – MAKE NO MISTAKE. ●

YOUR QUESTIONNAIRE

Having looked at some of the factors that can affect success or failure as a self-employed worker, here's a little self-assessment exercise for you to try out. Over the next three pages you'll find a total of 30 statements. Read each one carefully and measure how strongly you feel it reflects the truth for you. In question 1, for example, if you *do* feel that you work extremely well under pressure, put a cross through the circle labelled "7"; if you work poorly under pressure then your score should be closer to "1". For statements on which you have no strong views either way, mark "4".

The assessment shouldn't take you any more than 10 minutes to complete. Don't spend time agonising over a single answer – indeed, for the best effect, your answers should be as quick-fire as possible. And, of course, the whole thing depends on your answers being completely frank. The results of the assessment can be worked out on page 27.

Please bear in mind, though, that this is in no way an attempt at a serious, scientifically-based psychometric test. The outcome should only be treated purely as a guide, highlighting your general aptitude for the self-employed lifestyle, as well as pinpointing specific areas of strength and weakness.

1. **I work well under pressurised conditions.**   ① ② ③ ④ ⑤ ⑥ ⑦

2. **My health is very good – I rarely lose time though illness.**   ① ② ③ ④ ⑤ ⑥ ⑦

3. **I think of myself as being self-sufficient.**   ① ② ③ ④ ⑤ ⑥ ⑦

4. **I'm good at making decisions.**   ① ② ③ ④ ⑤ ⑥ ⑦

5. **My decisions are usually the right ones.**   ① ② ③ ④ ⑤ ⑥ ⑦

6. **I don't like being told what to do.**   ① ② ③ ④ ⑤ ⑥ ⑦

7. I stay calm under stress.

    ① ② ③ ④ ⑤ ⑥ ⑦

8. I work better outside of a team situation.

    ① ② ③ ④ ⑤ ⑥ ⑦

9. I actively enjoy assimilating new technology.

    ① ② ③ ④ ⑤ ⑥ ⑦

10. I like meeting people.

    ① ② ③ ④ ⑤ ⑥ ⑦

11. If a decision I've made isn't working I'm not ashamed to admit it and rectify it.

    ① ② ③ ④ ⑤ ⑥ ⑦

12. I'm a good communicator.

    ① ② ③ ④ ⑤ ⑥ ⑦

13. I can work with any type of person.

    ① ② ③ ④ ⑤ ⑥ ⑦

14. I enjoy learning new skills.

    ① ② ③ ④ ⑤ ⑥ ⑦

15. I'm a natural problem-solver.

    ① ② ③ ④ ⑤ ⑥ ⑦

16. I enjoy taking risks.

    ① ② ③ ④ ⑤ ⑥ ⑦

17. I'm focussed on my goals.

    ① ② ③ ④ ⑤ ⑥ ⑦

18. I hate it when I can't finish a task.

    ① ② ③ ④ ⑤ ⑥ ⑦

19. I accept that work will sometimes take precedence over my private life.

① ② ③ ④ ⑤ ⑥ ⑦

20. I'm a positive person.

① ② ③ ④ ⑤ ⑥ ⑦

21. People like working with me.

① ② ③ ④ ⑤ ⑥ ⑦

22. I'm a good listener.

① ② ③ ④ ⑤ ⑥ ⑦

23. I can take advice from others.

① ② ③ ④ ⑤ ⑥ ⑦

24. I'm not easily distracted.

① ② ③ ④ ⑤ ⑥ ⑦

25. I'm not scared of failure.

① ② ③ ④ ⑤ ⑥ ⑦

26. I can focus on a problem until it's solved.

① ② ③ ④ ⑤ ⑥ ⑦

27. I like to stand out from the crowd.

① ② ③ ④ ⑤ ⑥ ⑦

28. I have a clear, unequivocal set of aims.

① ② ③ ④ ⑤ ⑥ ⑦

29. Having made a decision, I act decisively.

① ② ③ ④ ⑤ ⑥ ⑦

30. I crave a sense of achievement.

① ② ③ ④ ⑤ ⑥ ⑦

YOUR RESULT

To assess yourself, total your scores over all 30 statements. Now see which group you fall into.

180-210

You are clearly a motivated person. You have a thirst for hard graft and are more likely to find that the levels of pressure and stress that come with self-employment are more likely to act as a spur to help you achieve your goals. As long as you have a sound business idea and properly plan your strategy you will succeed. Make sure that you don't get complacent about it, though.

One final question for you: were your answers truly a genuine assessment of your current attitudes, or simply what you would like them to be? Wishful thinking is not a useful trait for a new business venture.

130-179

You probably have a realistic view of your own capabilities and should be confident that you have many attributes that are geared towards success. But study the way in which your total is made up. Did you achieve it with fairly consistent scoring – mostly around "5" and "6" – or were there some statements for which your scores were unusually low? If so, pay close attention to them: they might help you identify areas in which you could benefit from improvement.

80-129

Scores in this range are likely to show a degree of uncertainty or a lack of self-confidence. As much as you might like the idea of working for yourself, there are clear indications that you might find

---

DON'T TAKE IT TOO SERIOUSLY

Your self-assessment test *really is* just a guide, so don't read too much into it. It aims to show how well suited your personality would be to dealing with the everyday business of self-employment. There are undoubtedly certain attributes, such as self-reliance, self-confidence, good communication skills, and an ability to handle stress and pressure that will make going it alone considerably easier. BUT IT'S IN NO WAY A GUARANTEE OF SUCCESS. The test makes no attempt whatsoever to appraise your business acumen or your technical proficiency. These are clearly two important determinants of ultimate success.

Above all, though, DON'T BE PUT OFF IF YOUR SCORES WERE LOW. If your dream is to run your own business, you should want to do whatever it takes to turn that dream into reality. You can *learn* to be a better communicator; you can *learn* to handle stress more effectively; and the more you put what you've learned into practice, the greater your confidence will grow.

---

some aspects of self-employment difficult. But these are not insurmountable problems. Get as much outside advice as you can before you finally commit yourself to any course of action.

UNDER 80

OK, this may not have been the most scientific of tests, but if you answered a majority of "1" or "2" scores, you're going to find self-employment a tough call – no two ways about it. But that's no reason to give up. If this is genuinely the direction you want to pursue, consider a training course of some sort before you take the plunge. This will give you a clearer idea of where your strengths and weaknesses reside. ●

(not) shooting yourself in the foot

Any of the statements in your questionnaire for which you scored lower than "3" could indicate areas of weakness that may affect your business. In this section we'll concentrate on natural tendencies, behaviours and practical issues that point towards failure, and how to stop them sabotaging your venture at the outset.

CLEAR DIRECTION

Without a clear set of measurable goals you won't be able assess your progress. It doesn't matter whether it's a simple statement of intent – "To work from home, put in no more than five hours a day, and earn as much as I did in my last job" – or a long and complicated business plan, if you know where you're heading it's easier to tell when things are going astray, and what corrective action needs to be taken. And it also allows you to take pride in having achieved the things you set out to achieve.

DISCIPLINE

Working on your own steam can call on huge reserves of discipline. If you are mercurial by nature, flitting from task to task as and when the mood takes your fancy, you'll have trouble surviving in business without some sort of mechanism for overriding those instincts. Keep yourself in check. Set daily quantifiable tasks and work on them until they are finished. Introduce a reward system if you find that sort of thing helps. This is a serious issue for many home workers, but it nonetheless needs serious addressing, otherwise your chances of ever hitting a deadline will be slight.

TAKING PRIDE

It's all about taking a pride in what you do. Every successful business has a set of core values that should define its standards. If you don't live up to the standards you have set yourself, you're certain to end up failing.

Every successful business has a set of core values that defines its standards

was
that
tting
little
in no
ed. I
even
ck as
ound
took
/e all
loody
ou to
come
I have
nts an
round
e, you
et in."

es with
marked
t when
t when
t when
ust to stir

...ctivities thrive on consistent behaviour. If the quality of your work or reliability shifts with your moods, you'll quickly get a "difficult" reputation. That's one of the worst things that can happen – and one of the hardest things to shake off.

LIFE IS SCHOOL

The term "knowledge economy" isn't just a handy categorising soundbite, it explains itself very succinctly. We depend on what we know: if we stop learning we get left behind.

Bill Gates is a voracious researcher. When he *really* gets into something he has to know as much as he can about it. According to his friend Ann Winbald: "To Bill, life is school. There's always something to learn." If that maxim is good enough for the most successful entrepreneur of the modern era, it ought to be for you.

COMMUNICATION BREAKDOWN

Communication is an essential part of life, and at the very centre of every business activity. If you don't communicate effectively, you can cause all kinds of problems. How are you going to "sell" yourself to clients? How can you give a brief? How can you instill a sense of confidence in others?

THE SECRETS OF SELF-EMPLOYMENT #2

Think of communication as more than what you say. Within 30 seconds, we know someone else's competency to within 80% accuracy

> **"** My main problem was playing it too safe. I always thought I was a poor decision-maker, cursed, as my wife says, with the ability to see both sides of any argument. Every conflict I've ever had to face I could come up with a balanced list of "fors" and "againsts" ... and when it comes to business I've always erred on the side of safety. I've lost count of the number of business opportunities I've missed through being so cautious. It used to frustrate me, but mostly because others would tell me how much more successful I could be if I took more risks. I read books, I did a couple of courses. I even saw a psychotherapist about it once. But one day I had my own Epiphany. It dawned on me that I'd been running a successful business for ten years built on the very idea of caution. This trait that I'd been trying to rid myself of is actually a defining part of my business. I've got to where I am by being who I am. And I'm happy with that. In my own terms that makes me a great success. **"**
> **James Burfield,** *import trader*

THE SECRETS OF SELF-EMPLOYMENT #3
Striking out on your own requires confidence in the first place. But there's no better way of breeding confidence than getting out there and doing your own thing successfully. Take one small step at a time, but acknowledge each achievement before moving on to the next.

If you're extremely shy, tongue-tied, poor with words or easily intimidated, you're going to have a hard time on your hands. These are by no means insurmountable problems, but you will have to work hard on improving your skills in these areas if you're serious about getting your business off the ground. There are many books, tapes, videos and courses that offer sound practical advice for turning around communications problems.

It may be similarly difficult for those with naturally confrontational personalities, or those that like to air their views in a forthright manner. The common sense advice is simple: try to tone it down. As hard as that might be to do in practice, when dealing with clients in most situations it pays to be as uncontroversial as possible. After all, most of us want a peaceful life, don't we?

What fatalists call a lucky break is just a seized opportunity to a pragmatist

KEEPING AN OPEN MIND

Keeping focussed on your goals is critical for maximising success, but don't let it blind you to what else is going on around you. Opportunities surface all the time, and you need to be open to all possibilities – however stupid they might appear on the surface. What fatalists would call "a lucky break" is merely a seized opportunity to a pragmatist – don't forget Louis Pasteur's famous quote: "Chance favours only the prepared mind." ●

BUSINESS SKILLS

The key areas that we've just looked are all behavioural in nature. But even if we were able to reprogram bad attitudes, there is a core level of basic business understanding that needs to be appreciated. On the right you can see the ten most common practical reasons why a commercial venture is likely to fail – and by failure we are not talking in any metaphysical sense, but in hard cash terms. At the end of the day, unless you are engaged a philanthropic enterprise, your business has to make money. Any of these factors will impede that aim.

It's not just personality traits that are being called into question, but basic business skills, knowledge of markets, and finances as well. Nobody can be an expert in all the different disciplines that you are likely to face if you become self-employed, but you need an appreciation of the ones that will affect the you most. For this reason, gaining an intimate understanding of the mechanisms of your own market is a fundamental necessity. If that isn't there before you start, you will face a struggle. Do as much market research as you can before making any decisions.

Let's finally look at the bottom line. "Working capital" is the finance needed to keep the business going between between paying suppliers and getting paid by clients and customers. All businesses go through sticky patches, especially during the start-up period, but when your working capital runs out you're in trouble. Quite simply, the more cash you have behind you when you start, the better your chance of surviving a crisis. ●

UNDERESTIMATING COSTS

FAILING TO KEEP FIRM CONTROL OVER COSTS

TAKING UNNECESSARY RISKS

LACKING SKILLS IN SALES, MARKETING, FINANCE OR IT

UNDERPRICING YOUR PRODUCT OR SERVICE

LOSING CONTROL OVER YOUR CASH FLOW

FAILURE TO GET CUSTOMERS TO PAY ON TIME; PAYING SUPPLIERS TOO QUICKLY

INADEQUATE UNDERSTANDING OF YOUR MARKET

FAILURE TO ADAPT YOUR PRODUCT OR SERVICE TO NEEDS OF CUSTOMER OR CLIENT

EXPANDING TOO QUICKLY

up
and
running

2

in this chapter...

but where do you start?

Having already concentrated on some of the more philosophical aspects of going it alone, let's now take a look at some of the practical steps needed to transform a business idea into reality.

GIVEN THE AMOUNT of our time it uses up, it would seem that many of us are pretty blasé about the fundamental issue of our day-to-day work. Although we may give periodic thought to career strategies, only a small proportion of us seem to do be doing a job that we *really* want to be doing.

Perhaps the problem is that we just don't ask ourselves enough questions. When was the last time you *seriously* queried whether the activities on which you spend upwards of 35 hours a week *really* constituted the most fulfilling use of your time (seriously enough to think about alternatives, that is)? If the only in-depth discussion you've ever had about your future working life was years ago with a school or university careers officer, you won't be alone. Indeed, the fact that it's been estimated that only around 15% of graduates end up working in their fields of study leads us to suspect that an astounding proportion of the workforce has little idea of what they *ever* really wanted to do.

OK, there's clearly a practical issue here. We all have to work if we want to achieve any more than subsistence living. But doesn't it seem amazing that so many people seem prepared to go along blithely with a job or career that just happens to have been the first one that came along?

Pretty well anybody is capable of doing pretty well anything

If that describes you, and you're happy with the way your working life has turned out, that's wonderful. If not, however, here's a reminder for you: IT DOESN'T HAVE TO BE THIS WAY. Think for a minute of the entire spectrum of human endeavour. With the right training, education and, above all, motivation, the truth is that pretty well ANYBODY is capable of doing pretty much ANYTHING. OK, we can't all be Picassos, Mozarts, Einsteins or Pelés, but beneath this rather special elite sits the vast majority – the likes of you and I. We know we probably won't ever be the world's greatest *anythings*, but we *can* be damned good at the things we *want* to be. If we really want it.

SO WHAT DO YOU REALLY WANT?

It may perhaps be that you are taken with the idea of the self-determination that goes along with self-employment, but are yet to come up with a clear way forward. Let's take a brief look at some of the options you might face.

SAME WORK; DIFFERENT SCENARIO

There are many full-time employees that basically enjoy the work they do. What they can't stand is the circumstances in which they're having to do it. Going solo offers the chance to continue your

> **"** Even when I was a boy I loved detective novels. I always used to tell my school careers teachers that I wanted to write for a living. They were not at all encouraging. I ended up with a successful career in insurance – in fact I was a finance director by the time I was 36. My life was so chaotically busy that I could never find time to write, but the dream never really went away. Two years ago, the company was taken over and I was given the choice of a pay-off or relocation in a junior position. Eight months later, at the age of 47, I had my first novel published. My income has dropped by about 80%, but I've never been happier. **"**
> **Harrison Dance, *author of "Same Sides"***

THE SECRETS OF SELF-EMPLOYMENT #4
You probably spend up to 70% of your waking hours at work, so why not use that time doing something that you really enjoy?

career on terms that are acceptable to you. You no longer have to put up with office politics, work alongside people you don't like, or spend your days in a environment you find repressive.

Besides the independence that self-employment brings, one clear advantage (if it's on your agenda) is that if you were to perform your existing "permie" job as a freelance contractor you would probably make more money. Furthermore, you are likely to gain a much broader experience more quickly than your permanent counterparts. As a result, your CVs is likely to be more wide-ranging than most, making you more attractive both to prospective clients and future employers.

A RETURN TO WHAT YOU DID BEST

Here's a story that you've doubtless heard or seen acted out many times before. It stars a Bright Young Thing, really passionate about a job that he does extremely well. So much so, in fact, that he quickly finds himself promoted out of it. ➼

> ❝I was a pharmacist until I was 51. But since my childhood my hobby had always been collecting crystals, rocks and precious stones. Twelve years ago I discovered the existence of a powerful East German camera lens that could be fitted to a microscope. I realised immediately that I'd be able to bring to life an incredible world of colour and form, and so I started to spend more and more of my free time creating magnified slides of my collection.
>
> Following a chance meeting at a photographic trade show, I sent a few to a magazine. The response was staggering. I decided to set up small sideline making them available to picture agencies. Within 18 months it had taken over my life. I handed the pharmacy over to my son and decided to become a full-time photographer. My work can now be found in picture libraries all over the world. They've been used on television, films, books, and even CD jackets. ❞
>
> **Gordon Anderson,** *The Small Picture Studio*

Unfortunately, he's not a natural manager. And he doesn't much like doing it. The problem is, going back to his old job means demotion and a pay cut. And management is always perceived as being the logical career progression, isn't it?

In fact, even if they were never star players, many successful (and effective) bosses never quite recapture the thrill of their pre-managerial careers. But pride can be a huge obstacle. Whatever reasons you give for "stepping down" there is always a danger of being written off as someone who just couldn't cut it.

Self-employment has several clear benefits to those who have been through this process. It allows a return to the kind of work that they know and love (although technology-oriented careers may require some retraining), but makes

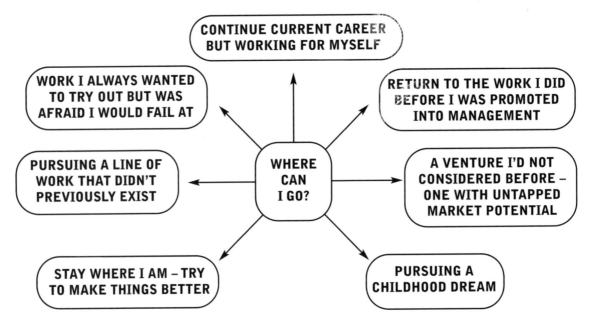

In need of a change? There are plenty of possibilities.

it possible to take that step back without the ignominy of having to return to the ranks.

Ex-managers are, in fact, among the group most likely to succeed in self-employment. Many will have a good deal of practical experience (and even formal training) in the many administrative skills needed to run a business successfully.

HOBBIES GALORE

Most of us have more than one set of marketable skills. In some areas, hobbyists have proved able to compete with the professionals. It's well known, for example, that as an amateur astronomer in the 1950s, Patrick Moore carried out work that was used extensively in NASA's early lunar projects.

It's only natural that in the search for a perfect life, our thoughts turn to leisure pursuits and childhood dreams. But there is a downside in turning a hobby into a business. Ask yourself if an activity that has always provided relaxation or a creative outlet will still fulfil these functions if you do them all day every day, and depend on it for your livelihood.

PLAYING SAFE

Many of us stay put in careers that are "just OK" for reasons of security. This usually breeds inertia – the longer that goes on, the harder it becomes to escape. This is no great surprise. Humans are creatures of comfort. Most of us favour consistency over unpredictability any day of the week. But this "safety net" can constrict our ambitions. There are a lot of people out there who could be living greatly enriched lives if they could put this fear behind them.

THE NO-LOSE MODEL

Fear of making the wrong decision prevents many of us from making fundamental changes to our lives. It's just that most us have been brought up in fear of making mistakes. We feel that we should be somehow be perfect, and forget that making mistakes is a vital part of learning. But as author Susan Jeffers says: "Our need to be perfect and our need to control the outcome of events work together to keep us petrified when we think about making a change or attempting a new challenge."

She suggests that we need to look at these issues from a different angle. We usually weigh up the pros and cons of each decision, but she calls this a "no-win model". This is because we focus on the "what-ifs" rather than the benifits. **Her "no-lose" model focuses only on the "goodies" of each outcome.** It teaches us that which ever way we choose, the outcome will be positive. If you take the fear out of decision-making your decisions will be all the more meaningful.

THE SECRETS OF SELF-EMPLOYMENT #5

One in six people considered starting up in business in the last two years, but only 2% actually did it in the last 12 months, due to financial fears*. Lose your fear and just do it.
*Source: Fear of Flying Report, Abbey National Business Banking

MODELLING FOR SUCCESS

Most of us can think of at least one other career possibility that we would like to try out if we could summon up the courage. Some of them may seem fanciful compared to our current circumstances, but we should NEVER write off any possibilities without at least a bit of thought. How do you ever expect to live your dream lifestyle that way?

It's easy to mock the guy working at the local video rental shop when he tells you that he *really* wants to direct his own films based on scripts he's already written — but that's exactly what Quentin Tarantino did. Or the young lawyer who wants to become an opera singer, even though he's blind and had no formal training — that's what Andrea Boccelli did. Or the the bank clerk who dreams of setting up a world famous motor racing team — that's what Eddie Jordan did.

Somebody out there is already living your dream – find out who they are

Does this sound like your sort of company? The truth is, unless you have come up with a career idea that doesn't yet exist — which is not really that likely — then someone out there is already living your dream. So find out who they are. Research as much as you can about these people. Read the biographies (or, better still, the autobiographies). And trawl the Internet for useful snippets. As long as your target is not an unapproachable celebrity, you could even try talking to them in person — successful people are usually proud of what they have achieved, and can often be unexpectedly free with advice.

The more information you acquire, the clearer the picture will be. What you are doing is building a "model" of those who have succeeded where you would like to follow. As management guru Peter Drucker points out, entrepreneurialism does not come from our genetic make-up. It's a discipline that can be learned. Modelling is all about looking at real-life examples and trying to discover the actions and behaviours that led to success. If you can do that, you can then use them to replicate similar results for yourself. This is as close as we can get to coming up with a formula for success.

> **"** I worked for the civil service for eight years – six of them doing much the same job. The four years before I plucked up the courage to resign were really strange. I knew my job backwards and could find no new challenges to get my brain going ... what's more, everybody in my team seemed to be the same. But the more soul-searching I did the further away a useful solution became. My big problem was that the work was just so easy, I was well paid, and most of my colleagues were also good friends. At times, going to work was more like going to a coffee morning!
>
> I've been self-employed for three years now. And, I have to say, that there are pressurised times when I wish I could just stroll into the council office like the old days. But what I enjoy is how my new life keeps me on my toes – there's no room for complacency when you know that every few months you have to start pitching for work all over again. **"**
>
> **Mark Ashwood, *planning consultant***

DON'T LOSE YOUR VISION

Don't let others put you off in your search for your ideal working life. You have a dream. It should excite you. You're bound to want to share it with the world. But don't be surprised if your idea is met with indifference or hostility – even among your friends. Now is the time you need to be stong. A newly developed idea can be an extremely delicate seed. If you're not careful it can easily be destroyed by a misplaced laugh, a shrug of the shoulders, a sneer or a waggish jibe. When people start threatening to jump ship at the office, it can be a disconcerting experience for rest of the crew. It can create uncertainty and even jealousy. It can bring out that "what's-so-special-about-you-that-you-think-you-can-be-different-from-the-rest-of-us?" mentality. Don't flinch. WHATEVER YOU WANT TO DO, THERE IS A WAY THAT YOU CAN DO IT. Now it's up to you to find that way.

THE SECRETS OF SELF-EMPLOYMENT #6

Success doesn't usually happen by chance. Look to the examples of those who have reached the top in your chosen field. Use modelling to figure out what it was about their behaviour that enabled them to succeed.

SOME FINAL THOUGHTS...

❝ Only those who dare to fail greatly, can ever achieve greatly. ❞
Robert F. Kennedy

❝ Our world has changed over the years because new ideas were acted upon. People may not have had all the answers, but as they began to take action, the answers became clear! ❞
Catherine Pulsifer

❝ The man with a new idea is a crank until the idea succeeds. ❞
Mark Twain

❝ Acting on a good idea is better than just having a good idea. ❞
Robert Half

❝ Daring ideas are like chessmen moved forward. They may be beaten, but they may start a winning game. ❞
Johann Wolfgang von Goethe

❝ Often the difference between a successful man and a failure is not one's better abilities or ideas but the courage that one has to bet on his ideas, to take a calculated risk – and act. ❞
Maxwell Maltz

❝ An idea can turn to dust or magic, depending on the talent that rubs against it. ❞
William Bernbach

❝ If I have a thousand ideas and only one turns out to be good, I am satisfied. ❞
Alfred Nobel

evaluating your idea

Whether it's taking your old corporate life into the world of self-employment, pursuing a hobby or plunging into a brand new venture, it goes without saying that you need to consider carefully whether the business idea you have chosen is a viable one.

STILL NO IDEAS?

Don't worry. It's quite feasible for a person to be passionate about the notion of leaving their old job and being their own boss, and yet still be clueless as to what form their business should take. It's logical that you have a greater chance of success if you use existing knowledge or skills, but that might not be the direction you're looking to pursue.

One approach you can try is "brain-storming". Get together with some sympathetic friends, colleagues or family and bounce ideas around. Write down every single idea that comes up – no matter how stupid.

You may be surprised at the number of winning business or creative ideas that have evolved from a semi-serious remark made over a few glasses of wine.

WHAT IS THE HALLMARK of a good business idea? That it's sustainably profitable. That's basically it. There are many would-be entrepreneurs out there who will never get off the starting blocks because they have a misconception about what a business needs to be successful. Does it have to be original? Did Sir Richard Branson invent airlines? Did James Dyson invent the vacuum cleaner? Did Bill Gates or Alan Sugar invent PCs? No, what they did was bring something new to an existing market. Being the first is actually *less* likely result in success since it's incumbent on you first to educate the market. Although the world would be a poorer place without pioneers like Clive Sinclair, you have more chance of success if you can build from a product or service for which there already exists a market, but at the same time, make yours distinguishable from the competition. ●

YOUR BUSINESS IDEA: 20 QUESTIONS

To test out the quality of your business idea, here are 20 very basic questions. They may not all apply to your own idea, but the more times you can tick the "yes" box, the more likely it is to succeed. Take this exercise seriously, though – the answers you give will go on to form the basis of your business plan.

Yes No

☐ ☐ 1. Have you defined your product or service idea?

☐ ☐ 2. Have you carried out any market research?

☐ ☐ 3. Have you worked out which market(s) to whom you can sell your product or service?

☐ ☐ 4. Is that market large enough for you to build a business idea?

☐ ☐ 5. Have you identified you target clients or customers?

☐ ☐ 6. Have you compiled a detailed profile – likes and dislikes, for example?

☐ ☐ 7. Have you identified how your intended product or service will benefit your client or customers?

☐ ☐ 8. Are you certain you can *really* fulfil that need?

☐ ☐ 9. Is your product different from competitors in the same market?

☐ ☐ 10. Have you estimated how much of your service your customers will buy? And how frequently?

☐ ☐ 11. Do you have a clear idea of how your product or service will be sold?

☐ ☐ 12. Is it a developing market?

☐ ☐ 13. Have you sounded out potential clients or customers?

☐ ☐ 14. Do they respond favourably to your idea?

☐ ☐ 15. Will the product or service you are offering live up to your intentions?

☐ ☐ 16. Have you set your price?

☐ ☐ 17. Have you estimated your business overheads?

☐ ☐ 18. Have you estimated profitability?

☐ ☐ 19. Have you assessed the primary risks in your business venture?

☐ ☐ 20. Will it provide you with an income you can live on?

your business plan

A good business plan is the most important document for anyone going into a new venture. Crucial to your success is having a set of measurable objectives. A good business plan describes your aims both in the short and long terms, along with realistic forecasts of your likely performance. A business plan gives you a focus for your goals, and can be used to convince others of your strategy.

MANY SUCCESSFUL BUSINESSES have been started and run on a "wing and a prayer". And good luck to them – it proves once again that there are few hard-and-fast rules in the world of small business. But this approach is not wholly advisable.

A good business plan details the scope of your ambitions and precisely how you intend to attain these goals

Having a good idea of how you think your business might progress is one thing, but fleshing it out with detailed figures is a different matter altogether. This is the very essence of creating a business plan. Think of it as a kind of "reverse CV" – instead of advertising your achievements, it details the scope of your ambitions and how you think you are going to attain these goals.

Many start-up companies make the mistake of only putting a business plan together when they need funding. In fact, going through this compilation process will help to clarify your thoughts, highlighting the steps you need to take to achieve success. Furthermore, when the business is up and running, it helps you maintain control by showing how your actual performance is matching up to your forecasts.

> ❝ Most people plan more extensively for a vacation than they do for a new business. Big mistake! ... If you take the time to plan all the steps involved in starting and running your new business, you are on your way to success. ❞
>
> **Edward Paulson, *business consultant***

HOW BIG SHOULD IT BE?

If you're finding the idea of creating a business plan daunting, don't worry too much. The amount of detail you need to include in your plan will largely depend on the size and scope of your business – and the amount of capital you are looking to borrow.

Massive multinational organisations looking for millions of dollars worth of funding may have business plans that go into several lengthy volumes, and take months of careful preparation. A small loan of less than £10,000, on the other hand, won't require too much detail – a business plan of 5-10 pages will probably be sufficient. You'll find a template for a small-scale business plan over the next few pages.

BUSINESS PLAN BASICS

Let's briefly summarise what a business plan is all about:

- Confirms on paper that your business idea is a viable one
- Identifies strengths and weaknesses
- Provides you with targets by which you can measure success
- Gives a concise outline of your goals and how you aim to achieve them
- Allows you to experiment with "what-if" scenarios without risking your business
- Provides a document for raising funds from outside sources.

FOR OUTSIDER READING

Of course, if you have a commercial proposal that requires funding to get off the ground, a business plan is a necessity. After all, a potential investor would have to be pretty stupid just to hand over the cash without some indication that your venture was going to be a sound bet.

For most startup businesses requiring finance, the first port of call is usually your bank manager. Here your business plan is your calling card: without one, you are unlikely to get a penny. A good business plan will give the reader a clear view of what your business is all about, estimated levels of profitability, and how confident he or she can be in your ability to achieve those targets.

In essence, you can look on your business plan as an important piece of company advertising. You're trying to sell yourself and your activities to some pretty important customers here, so you should put considerable effort into presenting it in as a professional a manner as possible. ●

THE SECRETS OF SELF-EMPLOYMENT #7

Of over 1,000 small firms in 1996, those that had strategic plans had 50% more revenue and profit growth than companies that didn't have one. *Source: www.businessplans.co.uk*

DRAWING UP A WINNING BUSINESS PLAN

Over the next three pages you'll find a template for putting together the perfect business plan. Your task is to fill in your own details against each point. Also shown on pages 46 and 47 are sample profit and loss and cashflow sheets. Although preparing figures can be tedious, these two sets of figures are particularly important in that they show that some thought has gone into the amounts of cash you are likely to have at your disposal over the first year of business.

COVER PAGE (1 PAGE)

- **Business name**
- **Period covered**
- **Name of the person who prepared the plan**

A: BUSINESS PLAN SUMMARY (2-4 PAGES)

- **Mission Statement** — Brief summary of what your business is all about. (no more than four paragraphs)

- **Company Objectives** — Bullet-pointed list of your business aims, both business and personal. This includes sales and profit targets, as well as non-financial aims — for example, to provide the highest quality after-sales service. (no more than a dozen points)

- **Market Summary** — Brief summary of the current market. (one or two paragraphs)

- **Product Summary** — Brief summary of your product or service and why it will succeed in the current market. (one or two paragraphs)

- **Profit Forecast** — Estimate of annual profits over the first five years. (one or two paragraphs)

- **Investment Needed** — Estimate of capital injection required and the financial prospects of return for potential investors.

B: CREDENTIALS (2-5 PAGES)

● **Past Performance**
Summary of previous financial performance (if not a new business), with an assessment of how relevant this is likely to be in the future.

● **Employment Background**
Profile of your employment record (and other key members of the business if necessary). This should be less a standard CV than an exercise in showing off your achievements. Detail academic background if necessary – if you have a degree (or higher), it's probably worth mentioning even if it's in an irrelevant discipline.

● **Management Credentials**
Reasons why you think will be capable of running your own successful business.

C: THE PRODUCT OR SERVICE (2-4 PAGES)

● **Product Description**
Description of the product or service (more detail than in the Business Summary). If technical support data is needed, include in an appendix.

● **Competition**
Brief outline of your main competitors, and description of why your product or service is superior or different, and why it is marketable.

● **Operational Details**
If you are selling a product rather than a service, provide full details of how it will be manufactured, by whom, and any specialist equipment or skills that are required in the manufacturing process.

D: MARKETING AND SALES (2-4 PAGES)

● **Market**
Outline of the market in which you will be competing. Detail its past performance and future growth.

● **Customer Profile**
Identify your likely customers or clients.

● **Sales Strategy**
The medium in which you intend to sell your product or service, how you intend marketing yourself and how it will be priced.

E: FINANCIAL (4-8 PAGES)

● **Forecast Summary** A summary of the forecast figures that follow.

● **Monthly Profit And Loss** Forecasts of your monthly profit and loss figures for the next year. Lay figures out in spreadsheet format (*see below*). Your monthly profit figure is your income minus your costs.

● **Profit Forecast** Estimates of total annual profit for the following four years.

● **Monthly Cashflow Forecast** Forecasts of your monthly cashflow for the next year (*see right*).

● **Cashflow Forecast** Estimates of monthly cashflow for the following two years.

● **Assumptions** The rationale to back up your forecasts.

● **Risk Analysis** Possible changes in circumstances that could jeopardise the achievement of your forecasts.

	A	May	June	July	Aug	Sept	Oct	Nov	Dec	Jan	Feb	Mar	Apr	Total
1		May	June	July	Aug	Sept	Oct	Nov	Dec	Jan	Feb	Mar	Apr	Total
2	INCOME													
3	TOTAL SALES	2012	4543	1234	1112	1766	1567	9788	4236	1567	8765	8765	1243	46598
4														
5	EXPENDITURE													
6	SALARIES	1200	1200	1200	1200	1200	1200	1200	1200	1200	1200	1200	1200	14400
7														
8	GROSS PROFIT	812	3343	34	-88	566	367	8588	3036	367	7565	7565	43	32198
9														
10	FIXED COSTS													
11	Rent	120	120	120	120	120	120	120	120	120	120	120	120	1440
12	Printing	130	130	130	130	130	130	500	130	130	130	130	130	1930
13	Telephone	75	75	75	75	75	75	75	75	75	75	75	75	900
14	Light/Heat	50	50	50	50	50	50	75	75	75	75	75	75	750
15	Insurance	90	90	90	90	90	90	90	90	90	90	90	90	1080
16	Transport	45	45	45	45	45	45	45	45	45	45	45	45	540
17	Postage	50	50	50	50	50	50	50	50	50	50	50	50	600
18	TOTAL FIXED COSTS	560	560	560	560	560	560	955	585	585	585	585	585	7240
19														
20	TOTAL COSTS	1372	3903	594	472	1126	927	9543	3621	952	8150	8150	628	39438
21														
22	NET PROFIT/LOSS	640	640	640	640	640	640	245	615	615	615	615	615	7160

Profit and Loss Forecast

Monthly profit and loss forecast.

	May	June	July	Aug	Sept	Oct	Nov	Dec	Jan	Feb	Mar	Apr	Total
RECEIPTS													
Total Sales	2012	4543	1234	1112	1766	1567	9788	4236	1567	8765	8765	1243	46598
Cash Invested	10000												10000
TOTAL RECEIPTS	12012	4543	1234	1112	1766	1567	9788	4236	1567	8765	8765	1243	56598
PAYMENTS													
Rent	120	120	120	120	120	120	120	120	120	120	120	120	1440
Salaries	1200	1200	1200	1200	1200	1200	1200	1200	1200	1200	1200	1200	14400
Printing	130	130	130	130	130	130	500	130	130	130	130	130	1930
Telephone	75	75	75	75	75	75	75	75	75	75	75	75	900
Light/Heat	50	50	50	50	50	50	75	75	75	75	75	75	750
Insurance	90	90	90	90	90	90	90	90	90	90	90	90	1080
Transport	45	45	45	45	45	45	45	45	45	45	45	45	540
Postage	50	50	50	50	50	50	50	50	50	50	50	50	600
TOTAL PAYMENTS	1760	1760	1760	1760	1760	1760	2155	1785	1785	1785	1785	1785	21640
NET CASH FLOW	10252	2783	-526	-648	6	-193	7633	2451	-218	6980	6980	-542	34958
CUMULATIVE CASH FLOW	10252	13035	12509	11861	11867	11674	19307	21758	21540	28520	35500	34958	232781

Monthly cashflow forecast: All incomings are grouped under "Receipts" all outgoings are grouped under "Payments".

PRESENTING YOUR CASE

Your business plan is as just as much a part of your own brand persona as your headed stationery, business card or website. As such you should take care in the way you present it to potential investors or financiers. Pay careful attention to the way you lay out the information. Make it easy to read: use a sensible typeface and avoid cramming too much information onto a single page. Finally, have the finished article bound in a neat folder. Remember, if your presentation is unconvincing then it might be assumed that you will be similarly unsuccessful when trying to woo potential customers. ●

❝ The thing that always surprises me is that when I ask for the reasoning behind some of the profitability estimates I get presented with I get the distinct impression that about half the people I see have stuck a finger in the air and plucked a number out of nowhere. However sound their ideas might seem, I can't give much support to someone who fills me with so little confidence. ❞

Mark Brown, *bank manager*

THE SECRETS OF SELF-EMPLOYMENT #8
A useful free guide that includes more detailed advice on creating a business plan is the DTI's booklet *Business Planning: A Quick Guide* (URN 96/971)

SOURCING FINANCE

Depending on what type of finance you go for, it's important to start doing your research as soon as you can, as some types of finance can take over six months to arrange and, importantly, you don't want to be forced – by time pressures – into taking finance that doesn't suit your needs.

WHY SHOULD ANYONE LEND YOU MONEY?

Any lender needs to be confident that your business has a strong chance of launching and succeeding. This sounds obvious but it's a point that is all too often overlooked. You need to put yourself in the lender's shoes, and ask yourself: "why would they want to lend me any money?" And approach any communication with this in mind.

SOURCES OF FINANCE

BANKS

Bank loans are generally the most popular form of finance for the self-employed. They can be relatively quick to arrange compared with other sources of finance.

Traditional banks are fairly risk averse. If you want to get money from a bank, the trick is to think like a bank. As well as wanting to lend money to a sound business, banks want to know that should the investment not work out, they will be able to recoup their money. This is the important difference between lenders and investors. With lenders, you have a debt that they want to be sure of reclaiming. Investors have a stake in the business – their interest is in returns, above and beyond what is earned in interest on a loan.

Knowing a bank's attitude to risk is important. Your business plan should reduce their perception of risk. They will want to check out your credit rating, so do this before they do and sort out any glitches.

The banks view commitment to the business in financial terms and will expect you to be putting up your own money. To safeguard their money, they will look at what you own, equipment, stock and property. It's important to consider your ability to repay the loan. You could face the possibility of losing your home, if this has secured your loan.

Banks have a range of loans. It's best to do your homework before applying to find out which one is going to be the most suitable for you. Most of them

THE SECRETS OF SELF-EMPLOYMENT #9

Banks will often want to charge you the set-up fee annually. Negotiate this as a one-off fee at the start tend to be 'term' loans, where the payments are re-paid over a fixed period of time. Like mortgages you can get fixed and variable interest rates.

REPAYMENT TERMS

All loans have different terms with varying lengths of repayment. Be sure to get a variety of quotes and be realistic about which terms you can meet. It sounds obvious but, as you generally have to start repayments immediately, it's as well not to borrow money before you need to use it.

VENTURE CAPITAL

A venture capital firm will have fund managers, working on behalf of the shareholders who invest in their company. Like any company with share-holders, they're interested in maximising their returns and minimising any risk. As venture capi-talists have a stake in the business, they effectively have a degree of control over it.

Corporate venture capitalists are suitable if you need large sums of money – £500,000-plus, but more usually £5 million and upwards. Although they're less risk-averse than banks, they are still extremely thorough and it's not unusual for it to take up to six months and a lot of work for a contract to be agreed. For most people, venture capitalists are more useful when it comes to expansion of the business.

ALTERNATIVE GRANTS AND LOANS

There are hundreds of these available. They are usually offered for very specific purposes, particu-larly where the government is looking to boost economic development. Getting a loan can be a lengthy process and bureaucratic. One of the best

BUSINESS ANGELS

A viable alternative to corporate venture capital and banks are business angels, who are often self-employed or small business owners themselves. They're still as stringent as the corporates but they do lend smaller amounts of money, £20,000 and upwards. The National Business Angels Network is the umbrella organisation for Britain's net works of Angels. They operate a matching programme via their website, www.bestmatch.co.uk

sources of information is www.j4b.co.uk, a web-site which has pulled together a large proportion of the grants and loans available. It explains how they operate, what criteria you need to fulfil in order to qualify, as well as helping you to source specific grants.

Another site worth checking is the government's Small Business Service, www.sbs.gov.uk. Here you can find details of the Government's Small Firms Loan Guarantee Scheme, which helps those unable to obtain conventional finance because of a lack of security or track record.

FRIENDS & FAMILY

Friends and family could be a potential source of finance. This can work well when you have a rela-tionship of trust already established. But this needs to be handled carefully. It's not unusual for rela-tionships to turn sour over disagreements on the business or use of the money. If you decide to go down this route, draw up a contract to formalise the terms between you.

OVERDRAFTS

If the type of business you're going into requires only minimal funding, it can be tempting to use your overdraft facilities. The suitability of this really comes down to how you manage your money. Unlike a loan which has agreed terms of repayment over fixed periods of time, the bank can and will call in an overdraft at any time they choose to. I wouldn't recommend using your overdraft as a loan if you can't juggle your finances to accommodate the risks.

KNOWING WHAT TO CHARGE

WHAT ARE YOU WORTH?

One of the most important aspects of your business plan is getting your pricing right. This can be a sticky area – we don't really have a culture that's comfortable about talking about money. People tend to feel embarrassed when talking about money and how much they want to be paid. Especially if you've come from employment, you probably only had to negotiate your salary once a year, if that.

CALCULATING HOW TO CHARGE TIME

Broadly speaking, you're going to be using your time in three different ways:

● bringing in new business and business development

● administration and general maintenance
● servicing the business you've brought in.

It's important to consider all three of these activities when setting your prices, as you need to charge enough to cover your business and living costs on the basis that only a certain percentage of your time will be spent servicing your clients.

Allow for this in your business plan. If you don't allow enough time in your initial projections to do these other activities, particularly sourcing new business and business development, you'll find yourself unable to balance meeting the needs of existing clients and getting new business in. The implications of this are that you'll struggle to meet your projected income and you'll end up working all hours trying and stay afloat.

REALISTIC COSTING

When you cost out a piece of work, it's important to factor in everything involved. If you're going to write an article for a magazine that would involve extensive research, then reflect that in your price. It's too easy to feel that you should only charge for times that you're physically with a client or writing an article.

You need to maintain a balance of confidence and good project management (see Chapter 5 – Keeping it together), otherwise you'll lose out financially.

People tend to feel embarrassed talking about how much they want to be paid

WHAT THE MARKET WANTS TO PAY YOU

You will have to balance earning what's necessary to cover costs and make an honest profit with what the 'market' wants to pay you. Research how much other people in your area are charging so you can get a good feel for where to pitch your price.

This is the time to be honest with yourself. Don't sell yourself short and understand the value of everything you do. For example, if you're a project manager, a key part in getting projects delivered on time is your ability to build good relationships with other people. If you excel at this, it makes you a more attractive prospect. Clients will pay for important points of difference.

MORE THAN JUST THE PRICE
Don't assume that you need to be the cheapest in order to get the business. Most people have this dilemma when they set up. In order to get the business in through the door, they want to offer an irresistible price.

This approach has two big downsides:

● at some point you'll have to put the prices up and then have to justify these rises – this can be harder than charging the fairer price to begin with.

● people won't appreciate the value of what you're offering, as price and perception of value are two sides of the same coin. They might well feel that your skills aren't up to the job.

Research shows that the more experienced sole traders charge more, not just because they are more experienced but because they feel more confident about naming their price. Rather than concentrating on cutting your price to beat the competition you need to concentrate on your brand and your ability to deliver on your service.

> **More experienced sole traders charge more, because they feel more confident about naming their price**

If you don't want to charge the cheapest price you need to make sure that your brand doesn't reflect that. Read more on branding on page 94.

CONFIDENT INVOICING
If you feel squeamish around the subject of charging people, it's likely that invoicing will make you feel awkward, too. You need to get over this quickly. Lack of cashflow is one of the biggest reasons for failure in self-employment.

That's not to say you need to be aggressive. But when the time is right, and you've both agreed that you'd like to work together, discuss costs, agree fees and importantly discuss terms.

Do you need to be paid upfront, within 10, 20 days, or on completion of the project? If it's a long-term project, can you manage without cash until the end, or do you need to agree interim payments? See page 112 on invoicing.

A Matter of Status

Before you begin trading, you must decide on the legal form your company will take. For a one-man-band, this amounts to variations on one of two basic choices: you operate as a SOLE TRADER or form a LIMITED COMPANY.

THE DECISION WHETHER to set yourself up as sole trader or limited company is primarily one of finance and personal liability. Don't worry too much, though – this by no means needs to be a major brain-teasing issue. When it comes down to it, the legal form your business takes will in many cases be dictated by the nature, size and scope of your work. Let's take a brief look at the implications of each option.

THE SOLE TRADER

This is by far the simplest route to getting yourself started. If you adopt this status there are very few legal complexities to worry about. The only real difference between being a sole trader and a permanent company employee is that instead of being taxed on basic earnings, the amount you pay is calculated on the basis of your PROFITABLE INCOME. This is effectively your total earnings minus your operating costs. Your personal tax allowances remains the same as if you were in permanent employment.

Since there is no legal need for your annual accounts to be audited, you don't have to hire an accountant to do your books (*see pages 144-147*): if you prefer, you can make declarations using a standard self-assessment form. Nevertheless, many sole traders do prefer to use the services of a chartered or certified accountant: it takes up less time; you are (in theory, at least) buying professionally measured competency; and the tax man is more likely to accept this authenticity. Above all, an accountant should have an understanding of the kind of legitimate business expenses you can claim.

By far the simplest route to getting started is to become a sole trader

THE SECRETS OF SELF-EMPLOYMENT #10

Most single-person small businesses, operate under the sole trader banner. It's quick and easy to set up, and involves minimal amounts of legal red tape.

RESPONSIBILITY

The most significant issue is that of responsibility. Legally, you ARE your business. This means that if you make a financial loss, go bankrupt owing creditors, or through professional activities find yourself prosecuted for negligence, ANY PENALTY YOU FACE WILL BE A PERSONAL LIABILITY. If you find yourself in deep water, not only could you lose your business, but your life savings or even the very roof over your head. Better watch out.

Don't be thrown by the term, though. A sole trader doesn't by definition have to work alone. He can employ staff and generally behave in the same way as any other business. It's simply that he takes all of the profits and personally bears all the risks.

PARTNERSHIPS

From a legal standpoint, a partnership is no more than a group of sole traders operating under the same banner. ➕

SOLE TRADER – HOW TO DO IT

For most freelancer workers and small businesses, operating as a sole trader is by far the easiest route to getting started. It really is a simple process.

1. TELL YOUR LOCAL TAX OFFICE All this takes is a CWF1 form – *Notification of Self-Employment*. You can get a copy of it from any tax office, or as a part of the Inland Revenue information leaflet, *Starting Your Own Business*. YOU MUST DO THIS WITHIN THREE MONTHS OF STARTING TO TRADE. They will notify you of your SCHEDULE D number – most employers will ask for this at some stage, so it's a good idea to put it on your invoices as a matter of course.

2. TRADING NAMES If you decide to trade under a name other than your own, you MUST print your own name somewhere on your headed notepaper. You can check with Companies House to see if your chosen trading name is already in use – take a look at www.companies-house.gov.uk for confirmation.

3. WORK PLACE If you've set up special work premises you need to check with the local Planning Officer that it complies with health, safety, fire and environmental legislation, especially if you expect to hire additional staff at any time. Your local council's help line should be able to provide you with the necessary information.

4. VALUE ADDED TAX Unless you think registering for VAT will be beneficial for your business, you don't need to worry about it immediately UNLESS YOUR INCOME IS EXPECTED TO EXCEED £52,000 OVER THE NEXT 30 DAYS. You can read about VAT in depth on page 148.

Each of the partners has to pay tax and national insurance on a legally agreed proportion of the company's net profits just as if they were sole traders. Although partnerships can be run on pretty informal lines, it's not a wise idea to operate in this way. Always get a formal agreement drawn up by a solicitor. Like a marriage, a flourishing business partnership can easily turn into a boiling hotbed of resentment and unpleasantness. At the very least, these points should be contractually agreed:

- **Name of the business**
- **Names of the partners**
- **Outline of business activities**
- **Date the partnership became effective**
- **Starting capital**
- **Profit split**
- **Details of individual responsibility**
- **Conditions: hours of work, benefits, holiday entitlement, etc**
- **Buy-out, retirement or death clauses.**

LIMITED LIABILITY PARTNERSHIPS

LLPs are a very new form of business entity. They combine the advantages of limited liability with the flexibility of organisation characterised by a partnership. Since members of an LLP are taxed the same way as partners this may be an effective way of retaining your self-employed status but with the protection of your personal assets. ●

> **❝** I didn't know anything about companies or that stuff. I phoned the tax office and told them I was setting up on my own and asked what I should do. They sent me a form to fill in and that was that. I became a sole trader in about 10 minutes. **❞**
> **Martin Hiles,** *plasterer*

LIMITED COMPANIES

THINGS GET A WHOLE LOT MORE SERIOUS IF YOU FORM A "LIMITED" COMPANY. Unlike a sole trader, who is treated as an individual, a limited company is a legal entity in its own right. As such, there are strict terms and conditions laid down by company law that have to be met both during the set-up and the ongoing running.

In the eyes of the law, a limited company is owned by its shareholders and run by appointed directors. By law, there must be two directors (one of which is the company secretary), a minimum of two shares, and at least one shareholder.

If that sounds daunting, don't worry. For most owner-managed limited companies, these legal niceties have little real meaning. In practice, the person running the business simply operates under the grand official title of MANAGING DIRECTOR. He or she is also the shareholder. The company secretary, who is nominally responsible for ensuring that all legal obligations are met, is typically a wife, husband, partner, friend or member of the family. He or she doesn't *actually* need to know anything about complex company law – they don't *usually* have to play any part in running the company. Most commonly, the "managing director" takes care of all aspects of the business, an accountant does the books and prepares an annual statement, and the managing director and company secretary merely sign them off.

LIMITED LIABILITY

So why call it a "limited" company? Unlike a sole trader, who is personally responsible for company debts, the shareholders who own the company are limited in their liability TO THE FACE VALUE OF THEIR SHARES. If the company has been set up with the bare minimum of two one-pound shares, this means that there is a maximum liability of just two pounds.

There are some conditions when this limitation becomes invalid. If, for example, a company carries on its business or takes credit in the full knowledge that it is insolvent, this is termed "wrongful trading". Under the 1986 Insolvency Act, directors acting in this way may find themselves personally responsible for the resulting debts.

At the lower end of the business scale, the liability issue can be a bit of a red herring. In practice, for example, a limited company run by one person would never be able to procure substantial credit on the basis of a ridiculously small share value. In such cases, most banks or finance houses would expect the managing director of such the company to guarantee loans personally. This means taking on board the same kind of full liability faced by a sole trader.

TAXATION

The tax situation for limited companies is also more complex. Operating a limited company will make you liable for two different types of tax. As managing director, you draw a salary, on which you are subject to the same tax rules as any other individual in permanent employment. That salary becomes one of your company's business expenses. At the end of the trading year the company has to pay CORPORATION TAX on its net profits.

The owners of a limited company – the shareholders – are only liable for debts to the face value of their shares

Annual accounts for a limited company should really be done by a professional. They will be much more thorough (and consequently costly) than for a sole trader, and must also be made public. Unless you *are* an accountant it's not worth the time and effort in dealing with this kind of thing. ●

JUGGLING TAXES

Figuring out what to pay yourself as the managing director of your own limited company can have important implications. If you choose to give yourself an artificially low monthly salary, your tax and national insurance contributions will be reduced accordingly – it may even be possible for you to avoid moving into a higher personal tax bracket. Attractive as that sounds, the downside is that it reduces your company operating costs, meaning that the profits on which you pay corporation tax will be higher.

This type of juggling exercise is one of the great mysterious arts of the small businessman. However, this can have far-reaching implications on other aspects of your life. Reducing your personal salary, for example, is also likely to limit the potential size of any mortgage or other loan you may wish to take out.

SETTING UP A LIMITED COMPANY

If you want to set up a limited company from scratch, get yourself psyched up for some solid British bureaucracy. A good place to start is with the Department of Trade and Industry's publication *Setting Up In Business: A Guide To Regulatory Requirements* (URN 98/763). Every new limited company has to be registered with Companies House. There are a number of critical documents that have to be submitted along with your application.

MEMORANDUM OF ASSOCIATION

This outlines the basic structure and aims of your company. To make life (very) slightly easier, you can buy standard Memorandum of Association forms from legal stationers.

ARTICLES OF ASSOCIATION

Since these describe company internal matters, such as voting-in new board members or issuing shares, they are largely irrelevant to one-man operations. But they are a legal requirement.

THE OTHER FORMS

Three further documents are required before you can make your application: FORM 10 contains the personal details of the directors and the company secretary, and the official location of your Registered Office; FORM 12 is a Declaration of Compliance – a statement that the company has been set up according to the statutes of company law; FORM 117 informs the authorities that you are now ready to trade as a limited company.

WHAT NEXT?

You send all of your completed documents to Companies House, along with the registration fee of £20. If you're in a real hurry you can get a same-day service for a fee of £100.

This is REALLY DULL STUFF, isn't it? Surely your time would be better spent actually getting on with your business rather than messing with irrelevant but necessary legal detail? Of course, one alternative is to get a professional to do the leg-work on your behalf – many accountants and solicitors specialise in this type of thing. But there is another solution…

DOING IT THE EASY WAY

Buy an "off-the-shelf" company – a limited company that already exists as a legal entity but is no longer operating. Such companies can be resold by registration agents (usually accountants or solicitors). It is so simple to organise that you can be up and running for business within a few days. What's more, it costs about the same as registering a new company.

All you have to do is exchange the existing directors' names for your own (and possibly make the Memorandum of Association pertinent to your own business). Of course, you'll probably end up with a name that you don't like, but that's no problem – you can change it for a fee of £10.

The whole process is simplicity itself. All you need to do is choose a name, sign some documents, hand over a cheque, and your agent will deal with the rest. No hassle. ●

SOLE TRADER VERSUS LIMITED COMPANY

In most cases, it won't be too hard to figure out which legal status is most appropriate to your needs. If you're a traditional "freelance" worker operating in a fairly risk-free environment, you probably have nothing to gain by forming a limited company, unless your net profits are particularly healthy, in which case there might be financial benefits. Here are some comparisons.

1. CREDIBILITY

Some believe that displaying the letters "LTD" after your name (a legal requirement for a limited company) gives some kind of business credibility.

The jury's out on this one.

2. ADMINISTRATION

In spite of what any recent government may claim, setting up and running a limited company can force you through layer upon layer of red tape. This becomes understandable when you consider that a one-man limited company with a small turnover is essentially treated much the same as one that employs hundreds of staff and generates millions of pounds in profit. By contrast, the bare minimum that a sole trader has to do is fill out a single form to make trading legal, and complete a standard self-assessment tax return form.

Being a sole trader has unquestionably lower administrative overheads.

NO CHOICE

For the past 20 years it has been common practice in the technology world to find specialist contract work through an agent. In such cases you may find yourself effectively forced to form a limited company. The agent acts as an intermediary, selling your services to an end client, and paying you a fee for the work you undertake on their behalf. By dealing with limited companies, agencies can legally claim that they are not employers as such, but are buying the services of a legitimate company. In doing so, they avoid paying employers' national insurance contributions – these are paid by your own company. This arrangement is currently under siege from the government's IR35 tax regulation. See page 109 for more information on this thorny topic.

3. DEBTS

It's simple: sole traders bear full liability; owners of limited companies have a maximum liability of the face value of their shares.

If your business requires external finance, and your bank is prepared to grant a loan without a personal guarantee, the limited company option may be a safer route. Sole traders should always be aware of the potential risks they face.

4. NATIONAL INSURANCE

Sole traders pay national insurance contributions in two ways. CLASS 2 contributions are a weekly flat-rate payment; CLASS 4 contributions are calculated as a percentage of your net profits. These give you all the standard state benefits, such as pensions for retirement or incapacity.

> 66 I was forced to change my status to limited liability when I started contracting through an agency. All the red tape did my head in. I'm sure I pay less tax than used to, but my accountants bills are now at least three times what they were last year. 99
>
> **Damon Howe,** *contract data analyst*

Unsurprisingly, the situation is rather different for limited companies. As a director, you are expected to pay the same CLASS 1 contributions as anyone else in full-time employment. These figures are calculated as a percentage of your salary. That rate is much higher than for the CLASS 4 contributions paid by a sole trader. It doesn't end there, though. The company itself is also expected to pay further contributions on your behalf. These are based on salary and must be paid irrespective of company net profits.

You will pay significantly higher rates of national insurance as a limited company.

5. TAXATION

Depending on net profits, after personal allowances, sole traders pay normal rates of income tax (10% start rate; 22% standard rate; 40% higher rate). As director of a limited company, your salary is taxed in the same way but based on the salary you draw. The company also has to pay corporation tax. This varies between 10% for profits of £10,000 or less, gradually rising to 20% for profits between £50,000 and £300,00.

Since corporation tax is lower than standard income tax at similar thresholds, directors of limited companies paying themselves low salaries should get away with lower tax bills.

6. DEALING WITH LOSSES

As a sole trader, if your business makes a loss, this can be deducted from future profits, or from other income earned during the current or previous year. On the other hand, as director of a limited company, your personal income tax is unaffected by the losses your company makes. It is only possible to deduct such losses from the previous year's company profits, or future company profits.

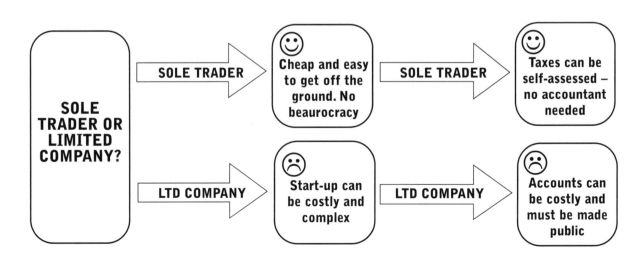

VALUE ADDED TAX

A scourge of the small business, VAT amounts to a form of tax collection carried out by the business world on behalf of the government. It is an "indirect" tax aimed at the final consumer. The current rate is 17.5%.

Irrespective of legal status, any business with annual sales of more than £52,000 MUST register for VAT. Any products or services sold by a VAT-registered company must include the additional VAT percentage; any goods bought from a VAT-registered business can reclaim the VAT element. VAT is collected on a quarterly basis – the total of the VAT reclaimed from purchases is subtracted by the total of the VAT charged on sales. The difference is paid to the government.

It is also possible to voluntarily register for VAT. This is not as insane as it sounds. If your business entails buying from VAT-registered companies and selling to VAT-registered companies it can reduce your operating costs – you can claim back the VAT on what you spend, and charge VAT over and above your usual fee – your customer or client will not be concerned because they will also reclaim the VAT that you have charged them.

VAT is covered in more detail on page 148-149.

If you are likely to make a loss at first, being a sole trader has greater benefits. If your business makes a loss while you are still in permanent employment, you are entitled to deduct those losses from your income, and claim a rebate on your PAYE income tax... as long as you can convince the taxman that your business is legitimate – he may well try to argue that running a part-time company at a loss makes it a hobby rather than a business.

7. PENSIONS

If your income is high and you want to make hefty pension provisions, a limited company will give you greater scope. As a sole trader the most on which you can get tax relief is 40% of your net profits.

A limited company can pay almost ANY amount into a pension scheme free of tax. This figure can even exceed the salary drawn from company funds. ●

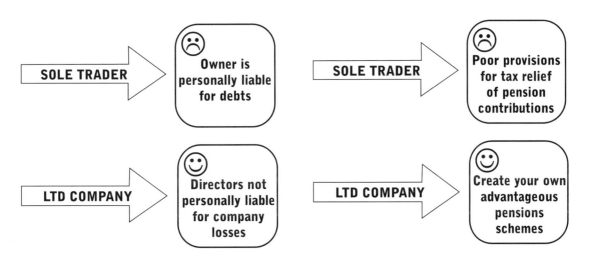

SOLE TRADER → Owner is personally liable for debts

LTD COMPANY → Directors not personally liable for company losses

SOLE TRADER → Poor provisions for tax relief of pension contributions

LTD COMPANY → Create your own advantageous pensions schemes

hitting the banks

In recent years, banks have come in for criticism from all sides in their treatment of the self-employed (and not without good cause), but whether we like it or not, they remain fundamental to any business. But although we may have to use them to carry out our everyday financial transactions, it's all too easy for us to forget that, as their customers, banks need us as much as we need them.

CHOOSING A BANK is a bit like going to a Mexican restaurant: although there seems to be a lot of choice on the menu, it all looks and tastes pretty similar. The adverts may hyperbolise new types of accounts that claim to be different from competitors, but when it comes down to it, as long as you can put money in and be confident

> **❝** In spite of what they might claim, some bank managers have considerable discretionary powers. If you don't like an aspect of the way your account is being managed, such as the way transactions are charged, make your feelings felt. Don't forget that as a consumer you have the ultimate power. If your bank doesn't provide you with the service you want, go and find one that will – there are plenty of them out there to choose from. **❞**
> **Mark Abram, *financial advisor***

that it will still be there when you want to take it out (not to mention the odd loan or overdraft), most of the high-street banks or building societies will do the job nicely.

The easiest way to check out the market is to trawl the banks in your locale. Walk into any one and you will find an array of brochures. If you compare the facilities on offer and the charges made you're unlikely to see a huge difference – but it is worth checking. Depending on the nature of your work, and your experience as a business person, it's also worth investigating whether the bank offers a small business advisory service. These can prove very handy for complete novices.

As a limited company, opening a business account will be your only option. The same is true of a sole trader operating under a business name. If, however, you are sole trader in business under your own name, you are likely to be better off opening a standard current account. This has the advantage of reducing charges and you'll also get a higher rate of interest (some business accounts offer NO interest at all on accounts in credit).

OPENING YOUR ACCOUNT

Most business accounts offer similar facilities:

- **Cheque book**
- **ATM card**
- **Paying-in book**
- **Monthly statements**
- **Automatic overdraft facility.**

Some banks also offer facilities for transferring cash or paying bills by telephone or the Internet. Some find these features gimmicky, others would claim that it's made their lives a good deal easier. You should, however, compare the costs of making electronic transactions with those of raising cheques. The banking sector is keen to encourage us to forget about old-fashioned cash and cheques, and sometimes offer financial incentives for doing so.

STATEMENTS

Like most regular personal accounts, every month (or more business account holders receive a statement outlining money which has entered or left their account during that period. Always check your statements thoroughly – mistakes DO get made. You really MUST retain your banks statements. Your accountant will want to see them when preparing your annual books. ●

REDUCING ACCOUNT CHARGES

Get into the habit of periodically checking the way your bank charges for its services. Although by law a bank must inform you of changes in conditions for operating your account, this information often comes in a form that bears a striking resemblance to junk mail. It can easily just slip through.

Business accounts typically incorporate standard charges for writing and paying in cheques, direct debits, standing orders and cash machine withdrawals. If your monthly business expenses are made up of a number of small, individual payments, you can reduce account-running costs by buying goods with a credit card or charge card. At the end of the month you can then make a single payment from your business account to clear your credit card. You will have to pay only one transaction cost. As long as each expense is accompanied by a separate invoice the source of the payment doesn't matter.

It's not actually necessary to have a formal company credit card for this purpose – any personal card you have will do. This is not a terribly bright idea, though. If you mix business and personal finance it's very easy to lose track of your spending and quickly wind up in a muddle. It needn't come to this. Credit cards are so easy to get these days – most credit companies are falling over themselves to find new cardholders. Life will be that much simpler if you get yourself a new card that you then use exclusively for business transactions.

Costs should play a significant role when you are deciding which bank to use. Don't forget to take a look at what building societies have to offer. Although their loan and overdraft facilities may be limited, if you are running a small-scale operation, their account maintenance costs are likely to be much lower.

your

work

place

3

in this chapter...

choosing the right space

There are some self-employed workers who are able to operate wholly from the premises of their clients. These are, in effect, temporary employees or "permalancers". Everyone else, however, is faced with a fundamental decision. Do you work from home or hire dedicated work space?

THERE WAS A TIME when the very thought of setting up a serious business from a spare bedroom in your home would have been met with howls of derisive laughter. How could potential clients or customers possibly take you seriously if didn't have proper business premises?

Well, the world has changed: technology has seen to that. As our economies drift further from a manufacturing base toward the service sector, the concept of the "virtual company" – one person and a laptop hooked up to the Internet – is now a universally accepted fact.

But although the idea of working from home is appealing to many of us, just because it's possible,

Just because you *can* work from home it doesn't necessarily mean that you *should*

it doesn't mean that it's necessarily the best way to conduct our businesses.

Some enterprises clearly require more space than just a computer and a desk – if you live in a one-bedroom flat, you may already be bursting at the seams. Equally, for those who view home as a sanctuary – a place from which the very idea of work is banished – finding outside premises will be a necessity.

One thing's for sure, you'll be spending A LOT of time in your office, so whether you stay at home or seek out dedicated business space, you'd better make it a comfortable space in which you're happy to spend your time. ●

SEPARATING HOME FROM WORK

When you're in permanent employment, it's easy to define the boundaries of work and leisure. When you are based at home, however, the two have a grim tendency to become blurred.

No matter how many critically important tasks you have to get through in a day, it's easy to get sidetracked by inconsequential domestic matters. Indeed, if it's one of those days when you don't really feel much like doing your work at all, then washing the dishes or sweeping floors can be a bizarrely tempting displacement – it's *sort* of work, isn't it? You're not *really* wasting time....

And then there are the inevitable interruptions from members of your household, "just popping in to see if you want anything". As well-meaning as they may be, it can break your concentration, and – as dictated by Sod's Law – will inevitably hit at the most inopportune moments.

THE SECRETS OF SELF-EMPLOYMENT #11
To minimise interruptions impose your own working hours, and make sure that everyone knows about them. If your family and friends understand that you're serious about your work then they're more likely to respect your wishes.

❝ When I first became self-employed I thought it would be really cool to work from home. What I didn't bargain for was the lure of videos, PlayStation and the Web! I'm in awe of those with the discipline to do it, but I gave up after three months and hired an office in a business centre – smartest thing I ever did! ❞
Jeff Edwards, *CAD technician*

How can you stop this happening? The first step is to ensure that your work space is kept as separate as possible from your living space. This has two important benefits: it keeps you away from people and things; and people and things away from you. If you're working at a lap-top on the kitchen table, then of course you're going to be tempted to do the washing up and eat toast instead of working; if you're in a dedicated office space then your distractions should be minimised.

In terms of size, industrial designers tend to allow for about 100 square feet per person. This is about the size of a typical spare bedroom: in an age where few homes have the luxury of a study, this has become a common alternative.

Once the room has been kitted out you should be able to shut the door and forget you are even at home. It's a two-way thing, though: think twice about allowing anything to escape from your office if it isn't leaving the house immediately. Don't let your work drift into your home space.

If you don't have a spare room, do your best to create a separate area in another room. You can keep the two zones apart using partition screens. But if your work tools are minimal you may be able to get away with packing them away each night. ●

WORKING FROM HOME

It's just another day trying to get to work: you're stuck in rush-hour traffic, sardined in a carriage in the mid-summer heat, dashing between the tube station and your office in torrential rain. You know the deal. At times like these, thoughts turn to employment Nirvana – the luxury of working from home. There's no question that the idea of a 30-second journey to work is an appealing one for many, but it does have its potential drawbacks.

HOME WORKING: THE GOOD BITS

Here are some of the advantages from working from your home.

TIME AND PRODUCTIVITY

● For most people, the journey to an outside office is wasted time. Some hardcore commuters can save up to four hours a day by staying home.

● Since you are most likely to be working in isolation at home, lack of interruption should make your time more productive.

SAVING MONEY

● You already pay the rent or a mortgage, or own the property, so there is no extra cost.

● Any expenditure on the "business" area of your home will be tax deductible (as long as it is used solely for work).

● Reduces your travel expenses (and probably the amount you spend on lunch).

FAMILY AND HOUSEHOLD BENEFITS

● Closer vicinity to your family. (You might even be able to get them to help you out from time to time.)

● Makes home less susceptible to break-ins.

THE LONELINESS OF THE SHORT-DISTANCE COMMUTER

When you're locked away for hours on end working in your spare bedroom/office, you can easily feel isolated – especially if you are used to the bustle of a busy office. Although working without interruption can be productive, it can also turn into cabin fever. You know you've got it bad when you notice yourself ranting about the minutest mundane detail of your day to any poor soul who pretends to listen. This is not a good state to be in. And it sets you well on the path to becoming a sad git.

One way to avoid this is to build a network of people in a similar position as yourself. Start by seeking out other self-employed people in your area. Even if you just drop in for a coffee a few times a week, it's human interaction, and that's nearly always healthy.

You can take things further by starting up meeting or dining clubs. Begin by inviting one or two self-employed acquaintances for a lunchtime drink, and ask each of them to bring a self-employed friend of their own. An entire network can quickly bloom in this way.

Of course, as well as being an excellent way of forging new friendships, there's always a chance that useful new business contacts may also blossom.

TESTING THE WATER

● Setting up an independent office usually entails a fixed-term legal commitment. Working from home allows you to try out your ideas without these obligations. You can always move later if you need to.

FREEDOM

● Freedom to work in any style that suits you. If you want to stay in bed and do your work on a laptop, you can; if you want to work with the all-day sports channel blaring out of your TV, you can; if you feel like taking a bath at eleven in the morning, you can.

● Allows for a more integrated life.

● No dress codes. ●

THE SECRETS OF SELF-EMPLOYMENT #12

If you can't spare around 100 square feet for home office space, looking for outside premises might be a better alternative. Shoe-horning yourself into a tiny space will end in frustration: your office will be inadequate and your home will have been compromised.

HOME WORKING: THE BAD BITS
But it's not all idyllic…

● Self-discipline is a necessity. When you're at home you can easily get side-tracked by your surroundings. Work displacement is also a threat – you know that's happening when you start to fool yourself into believing that that doing the washing up is actually "work".

● Isolation can be a serious problem for some people. Even if you work alone, renting office space rather than working at home is likely to bring you into contact with other people. Many of these will also be self-employed or business owners, so they may also be able to provide you with leads, business or guidance, as well as an occasional cup of coffee and chat.

● For some people, making a strict distinction between work and leisure is necessary to get the best out of both worlds. The time taken to commute between home and office is sometimes useful to emphasise this distinction. It's almost as if they use this space to psyche themselves up for the day ahead.

● Home offices can all too often spill out into the rest of your environment, creating the impression for you and your family that there is no escape from work (and maybe each other). As well as being a pain to those around you, it can also devalue the important idea of your home as a place to rest and relax. This is why if you do choose to work from home it's critically important that you strictly define work areas. ●

IS IT LEGAL?

Although basing your business at home has clear benefits in terms of saving money, there are a number of implications that you should take into account before making a final decision.

RESTRICTIVE COVENANTS

Even if you own your property, you don't necessarily have the freedom to do anything you want with it. On close inspection, the title deeds may incorporate what are termed "restrictive covenants". These are legal stipulations placing limitations on what practices are allowable on your land. This could prevent you running a business (or specific type of business). If your deeds contain such clauses, consult a solicitor who will advise what kind of action you can take.

MORTGAGE TERMS

If you are in the process of buying your home with a loan from a bank or building society, you really need to check the terms of your mortgage agreement. You may find that some – particularly those offered by the larger organisations – may specifically disallow commercial usage.

In practice, this merely aims to prevent "cheap" home mortgages being used for situations where a more expensive business loan would otherwise be offered. Anyone running a small business from a spare room, is very unlikely to run into problems with their bank or building society.

> **If you run a small business from a spare room, your mortgage lender is unlikely to be that concerned**

CAPITAL GAINS

If you claim a proportion of the costs of running an office from home as a part of your regular business expenses, you may pay find yourself penalised when you come to sell your property. This will mean that you may have to pay capital gains tax on the same proportion of the gains realised as deductions. A small gain may fall within your exempt allowances for any one year, but if in doubt, discuss things with your accountant.

LEASE AGREEMENTS

Similarly, if you rent your home, check that the terms of your lease don't stipulate that you are not allowed to run a business. If there is such a clause, before you go to the trouble of engaging a costly solicitor, make direct contact with your landlord. If you outline your intentions in a reasonable manner you may find that there are no objections. Failure to do this may void your lease, giving the landlord the legal right to evict you.

INSURANCE

Every sane person has a household contents insurance policy. But you should be aware that any item in your home subject to commercial use of any kind is unlikely to be covered under a regular domestic policy. What this means is that that your computer and other office equipment and furniture may need to be insured under a separate business agreement, or at the very least an extension to your existing policy.

PLANNING PERMISSION

Although most domestic offices are unlikely to fall into this category, you may find that running your business from home contravenes town planning regulations – council officials might argue that you've made a "material change in the use of land". In such cases you will have to apply for planning permission before you can begin trading.

Although all applications must fulfil strict legal requirements, planning committees have a good deal of discretionary power. Within residential areas, a simple "change of use" is likely to be approved as long as you can give assurances than you won't be creating noise or smells that upset your neighbours or the surrounding environment. Permission may also be qualified by strict conditions relating, for example, to the hours or times that you are allowed to work, or the number of visitors that you attract – especially in areas where street parking is problematic.

A fee is payable with your application. It is not refundable if you are refused permission. Contact your local council for copies of the relevant documentation.

In any case, you should check your policies carefully, or talk to your insurance broker, since you may find that operating an undisclosed business from your home may invalidate your buildings insurance – and that's a risk nobody would be advised to take.

IS THIS ALL *REALLY* NECESSARY?

Don't tell anyone you read it here, but the truth of the matter is that the vast majority of home-based small businesses and self-employed workers manage to operate inconspicuously without having given a minute's thought to any of the above legal points. And so long as they are not causing a nuisance to their neighbours or contravening environmental health or safety regulations, and they keep a low profile, then the chances of the relevant bodies finding out are slim.

This is by no means suggesting that you *should* ignore any or all of these factors. Indeed, if your business is to be totally above board they should all be taken into consideration where relevant. As ever, the decision's all yours.

A FINAL WARNING

Insurance is really another form of gambling. As such, you should never risk losing what you can't afford to replace. Ignoring business cover is, to say the least, foolhardy. If your work means that your home is filled with costly technology which you are unfortunate enough to lose in a fire or flood, or is stolen, then you may have trouble convincing your insurer that those items represent legitimate household contents. ●

THE SECRETS OF SELF-EMPLOYMENT #13
After 20-60 minutes, the brain becomes drained of oxygen and needs a rest. Set up an office that allows you to relax, too.

PLANNING YOUR OFFICE

For many of us, our surrounding environment takes a back seat: we're often too busy to worry about such things. But this can be short-sighted. With careful planning, offices can be designed to create a more effective working atmosphere.

> **❝** It's so important that you actually enjoy your surroundings. When I took over my office it looked like something out of a 1970s furniture advert – it was all terrible shades of brown and beige. I tried working with it for a couple of months, but ended up hating being there so much that I actually turned down work just so that I could find time to redecorate! **❞**
> **Roger Eyde,** *account executive*

OFFICE LAYOUT

Begin by drawing up a list of the furniture that you need in your office. As a bare minimum, this is likely to include a desk, chair, lighting and some sort of filing system.

Now it's time to decide where to everything should be located. To begin with, take a pencil, ruler and some graph paper and carefully draw the shape of your room. Although it doesn't have to be pin-point accurate, it should be broadly to scale (a ratio of 1 foot:1 inch would fit on most sheets of A3 paper).

From another piece of graph paper, cut out shapes (to the same scale) that represent the items of furniture and equipment. Label each piece. By positioning your cut-outs on the room outline you should be able to come up with a layout that works for you.

SOME THINGS YOU CAN'T (OR WON'T) CHANGE

As you prepare your layout, try to take into account the fixed elements of your office, such as the position of the door or the windows. Drafts and direct sunlight can affect both your health and performance: drafts can cause general discomfort and unpleasant muscle pain; if your desk is badly positioned, sun rays can create harmful glare on your computer screen.

Programs like KeyCad can be used to help you plan your office

Don't forget to mark the positions of the power points and telephone connections: with good planning you should be able to prevent the need for untidy or dangerous extension cables to be draped across the room. If your perfect layout does require additional cabling, make sure that it always follows the walls. Never leave loose cable laying across the room – someone is guaranteed to trip over it. Of course, if you're going to be *completely* professional about things, it's not exactly the toughest job in the world to relocate wall connections – although, as with all electrical business, if you're not completely confident in what you're doing, get an expert in.

COMPUTER DESIGN

If you are technically inclined, you can work out your office layout on your computer screen. You can use either standard graphics software or a specialised Computer-Aided Design (CAD) program (*see left*). ●

THE SECRETS OF SELF-EMPLOYMENT #14

Sitting puts 50% more stress on the body than standing. Be sure to invest in ergonomically designed furniture

COLOUR AND SPACE

What colour scheme do you intend to employ in your office? If your answer is "whatever's already there", then you might want to think again. There is a growing view that the colours surrounding us in our workplace can actually have an impact on the way we perform.

It's long since been known that colour can affect our moods and behaviour. In the early part of the 20th century, Rudolph Steiner claimed that school children behaved differently depending on the colour of the classroom walls. Swiss psychologist Max Luscher later showed that different colours could alter metabolic rates in human beings. Over the past decade, the concept of colour therapy – using colour to treat health conditions – has gained currency.

Most theories refer to groups of colours as being "warm" or "cool". Warm colours include red, orange and yellow; they can create a cozy, inviting and comfortable atmosphere. Cool colours include shades of of blue, cyan and sea green; these are more likely to produce a calm and peaceful atmosphere. Although many people choose plain white for a supposedly bright and spacious working environment, proponents of colour theory would argue that this not ideal for promoting a creative atmosphere.

Of course, if that sounds like a load of New Age nonsense you'll probably be better off surrounded simply by colours that you enjoy.

Colour also plays its role in the ancient Chinese practice of Feng Shui (pronounced "fung shway"). According to devotees, the flow of positive energy can be channelled through our surroundings according to the way furniture and other objects are positioned. The belief is that if the rules of Feng Shui are obeyed then our health and wealth will be maximised – which can't be a bad thing. You can find more about Feng Shui at www.fengshuisociety.org.uk.

WEB CONTACTS

www.ikea.co.uk	**General**
www.habitat.net	**General**
www.muji.co.jp	**General**
www.johnlewis.com	**General**
www.viking-direct.co.uk	**General**
www.christopher-wray.com	**Lighting**
www.ryman.co.uk	**Filing**
www.hag.no	**Seating**
www.space2.com	**Desks**
www.hmeurope.com/shop	**Seating**
www.back2.co.uk	**Seating**
www.thebackshop.co.uk	**Seating**
www.ergonomic-computing.co.uk	**Desks**

OFFICE FURNITURE

The office essentials are a desk, seating, lighting and storage. You may be surprised at the variation in quality and price available, so here are some tips to bear in mind when you are preparing to shop.

DESKS

A good desk should be practical, safe and attractive. Before you go shopping, make sure that you've measured the maximum space that fits into your layout. You can pay anything from under £30 to over £2000 for a desk, depending on design and materials used. Although most of us like to spend as little as possible wherever we can, before you go with the cheap and cheerful option, it's a good idea to look at the thinking behind some of the more exotic models.

First, though, give some thought to what you actually expect to go on at your desk. You might want space for a computer system, telephone and an area for spreading out your papers. Also try to be realistic – if your dining room table regularly turns into a pile of bills, newspapers and other rubbish, then it's a good bet that your office desk is likely to follow suit, so you'll want to make some space for a desk organiser.

Traditional desks are usually little more than rectangular lumps of wood (or MDF) on four legs. If you're on a tight budget, the cheapest of these are the flat-packed varieties you find in stores like Ikea and Habitat. Made from cheap fibreboard, they're not terribly strong, and will probably be sufficient only for most undemanding of users.

Things become more complicated if your work centres around a computer. A standard desk is only 80cm deep – to accommodate a computer monitor you need at least an extra 20cm. Many home workers choose integrated desk systems, which include shelves, drawers and multiplatform areas for computers and monitors all within a single unit. For those with a bigger budget, there are some amazing "wraparound" interactive systems available. The best models are designed around the way the human body works, minimising awkward

> **❝** People are usually bad at thinking out what they do and what they use. They just make assumptions, then buy something because it looks nice. What most people find when they work at home is that they start multi-tasking at their desks. As well as work-related papers, they have things like gas bills clogging up the space. **❞**
> **Andrew Baird,** *ergonomist*

or unnatural stretching movements. You can check out some of the best systems on the web (*see* left).

CHAIRS

There is a plethora of poor, cheap office seating on the market. FOR YOUR BACK'S SAKE, AVOID THESE AT ALL COSTS. Since you're likely to be sitting in your office chair more than any other, it makes sense to buy something substantial. Be warned, though, you can expect to pay at least a few hundred pounds for something usable.

> **❝** If you're going to invest money in your home office, even if you only have a small budget, the most important thing is the chair. **❞**
> **Nigel Heaton,** *ergonomist*

Ideally you should choose a chair that provides support for your back, allowing it to remain in its natural 'S' Curves, and can adjust to your own unique body shape. This means that both the height and backrest should be adjustable. In a good chair, the seat will be tilted downward slightly, reducing the pressure on the hips. Finally, if you spend long periods using a computer mouse you should really consider a chair with adjustable armrests. This takes pressure away from the the wrists, and so should minimise the risk of Repetitive Strain Injury (RSI).

The award-winning *Aeron* chair, manufactured by Herman Miller, is widely reckoned to be the most desirable office seating of the past decade. It uses a made-man fibre called "pellicle", which allows the body to breathe, and cuts the build-up of heat and humidity. It looks cool in a hi-tech sort of way, but the downside is that it'll also leave you with a handful of change from £750.

LIGHTING

Poor lighting is one of the biggest causes of both headaches and eyestrain among workers. This becomes exacerbated by long periods spend in front of a computer screen. Although there are quite a few theories on office lighting, most seem to agree that the most desirable state is to have a good source of natural daylight and then supplement that with artificial lighting.

As a bare essential in most small offices, the central ceiling light should be fitting with at least a 100-watt bulb. For detailed paperwork, a desk lamp is better for the eyes, and aids concentration. You can pay as little as £20 for simple angle-poise lamp in any department store; for the design-conscious, the classic Richard Sapper Tizio desk lamp can be acquired if you have a spare £200 or so. Wherever possible, though, consider using halogen bulbs – they provide powerful lighting at nearly half the cost of a normal light bulb. ●

THE SECRETS OF SELF-EMPLOYMENT #15

Be prepared to spend more than you might have expected on a desk and chair. Ergonomically designed furniture will help you to work more efficiently and will also reduce the likelihood of back injury. It'll also look much better.

FINDING AN OFFICE

Once you've made the decision not to work from home (or have had it made for you), you're faced with the potentially daunting prospect of finding business premises. As you will quickly discover, there are many different kinds of office space on the market, so by considering some basic factors you should be able to refine your search.

LOCATION

Begin by asking yourself what would be the ideal area for your work to be situated. To some degree this will be dictated by the nature of your business if, for example, you depend on being in close proximity to your customers or clients, or require access to roads, railways or airports. Some types of business may also feel they can benefit from operating in a prestigious area or postcode. Otherwise, since the journey to work is what most of us hated so much about permanent employment, it would be reasonably sensible to look for premises close to home.

COSTS

Try to get a feel for how much of an overhead you are prepared to pay for your premises. This includes your rent, business rates and day-to-day running costs.

> **❝** Try to get the premises first. I've run out of space and am trying to build extra capacity. My tip is to plan and make sure you have enough money behind you, because it gets used up very quickly. **❞**
> **Bill Stevens,** *apiarist (beekeeper)*

THE SECRETS OF SELF-EMPLOYMENT #16
Get two Internet Service Providers – then, if one goes down, you'll be able to work online with the other

If you are setting up in a designated government enterprise zone, you can avoid paying business rates at all. Other initiatives include Assisted Area status, for which you may be able to get an enterprise grant of up to 15% of your capital costs. You can find more about this at **www.dti.gov.uk/assistedareas**.

SIZE AND LAYOUT

You will already have some idea of how much space you need to operate your business. But if you're ambitious and already have an eye on future expansion, ask yourself whether you want to allow for that in these premises.

APPEARANCE

Are customers, clients or suppliers going to visit you in your office? If so, you need to think seriously about the appearance of your office (and perhaps surrounding area): they may have an impact on your image or credibility, especially if you work in visual areas such as art, design or architecture.

If you depend on visits from customers, you must also ensure that your premises are easily accessible by road and public transport. This means making sure that there are adequate parking facilities. ●

WHERE TO LOOK

It can be as difficult locating satisfactory working premises as finding a nice place to live – and in many areas your choice will be more limited. The The best advice is simply to keep your eyes and ears open, but some other sources are shown below.

● Local newspapers.

● Talk to local businessmen or self-employed workers operating in the same field as yourself – they will often hear about space before it comes onto the market.

● Find out which local estate agents deal with commercial properties. This is the most common way of finding premises.

● Local Business Link or enterprise agencies often have lists of vacant commercial properties within their region. They should also be able to advise you on the subject of grants.

● Your local council is also likely to keep a similar list. Buying or renting disused public buildings has traditionally attracted those in search of a bargain. ●

SMALL BUSINESS CENTRES

Many of Britain's larger towns and cities have specially designed small business centres. These are usually large office blocks or old factories that have been converted into small units.

Among the advantages they able to offer are shared services, such as a provision of manned reception area, telephone answering, secretarial facilities and security.

Operating from such a base also enables you to mix with other self-employed people. This can be of extremely useful in both social and business senses.

For hi-tech small businesses, similar arrangements may be found in "science parks", which are often linked to university research departments.

YOUR CHECKLIST (PAGES 76-77)

When checking out vacant premises it's not always easy to keep your mind tuned to the small details of your requirements. To make life a little easier, over the next two pages (76-77) you will find a checklist covering most of the practical details that you will want to consider. You might find it useful to make a set of photocopies of these pages. Each time you visit a new space you can fill in a new set of details. On the top right-hand corner of the sheet you'll see a place for you to make a sketch of the existing layout. Draw in the main shape and all the important features, such as doors and windows. A checklist like this will be an invaluable memory jogger when you make your final decision.

Ultimately, even if the space fulfils the needs you've identified, the deciding factors are likely to be less tangible. Finding an office is like seeking out your ideal home. If you have even the slightest reservations, or the place hasn't got the right "vibe" for you, then think twice about moving in. ●

FINDING PREMISES: YOUR CHECKLIST

ADDRESS...
....
....
....

AGENT...

1. SPACE

Office space ....

Storage space ....

Factory space ....

Selling space ....

General comments ....
....
....
....
....
....

2. APPEARANCE

Design quality ....

Appropriate for clients ....

Work required...

General comments ....
....
....
....
....

3. ENVIRONMENT

Light ....

Noise ....

Hygiene..

Safety...

Natural daylight...

Neighbours ....

General comments ....
....
....

4. FACILITIES

Telephone/ISDN lines ....

Computer network ....

Burglar/fire alarms ....

Heating...

Partitions ....

Power points..

Air conditioning ....

Kitchen facilities ....

General comments ....
....
....

SKETCH OF LAYOUT

5. ACCESS

Parking ....

Delivery facilities ....

Pedestrian access ....

Security systems ....

Near buses/railways ....

General comments ....

....

....

....

6. COSTS

Rent (per m^2) ....

Length of lease ....

Business rates ....

Maintenance ....

Running costs ....

Rent reviews ....

Payment terms..

Insurance arrangements ....

Fittings needed ....

Estimated decoration costs ....

General comments ....

....

....

GENERAL IMPRESSIONS

critical
technology

There can be no wimping out on this one. To compete in the modern business world you need to be "techno-literate". End of story.

IT MIGHT BE A CURIOUSLY British trait, but some people seem to take a perverse pride in NOT being able to deal with technology. Video machines are a good example: surely they're just simple tape recorders that follow a sequential set of instructions, aren't they? And yet to hear some people talk you'd think a PhD in quantum physics was needed just to record *Coronation Street*. Well, here's the news: THIS IS THE 21ST CENTURY:

THAT WON'T WASH. There can be no place for "technofear" in the modern world. Your mantra should be: "TECHNOLOGY IS MY FRIEND".

This is a serious point. The astonishing developments which have taken place in personal computing have helped to create a world that only a few years ago would have seemed unfeasible. Two decades ago, an average university computer

TECHNOFEAR – IT'S JUST A MATTER OF CONFIDENCE

ANYONE can get satisfactory results from most types of computer software within a few hours of switching on.

Throw away the user manuals They contain too much information. Instead, buy a "Dummies"-style software guide that takes you through the basics step by step.

Ask questions Many people are embarrassed to show that they are not computer-literate. We can't all be great at everything, so never be afraid to ask for help.

Don't panic Although some would claim otherwise, computers are painfully logical. When things go wrong, stay calm, and retrace your steps.

Take it easy You can only take in so much. If you spend any more than about four hours learning in a single day, you won't be able to retain all of the information. It's much better to learn in small blocks. You should also always try to put what you learn into practice as soon as possible.

department would have needed a "mainframe" the size of a small house to perform calculations that can now be handled by a spreadsheet. Little more than ten years ago, books were being physically typeset, each character being positioned on huge printing plates; this book is being written on an Apple Macintosh using QuarkXpress desktop publishing software. When it's done, the computer files will generate the film from which the printing plates are made. And as for the Internet, has there been a more important development in the field of human communications since the birth of television?

Not all of us can be computer wizards, but you should at least aim to be "techno-competent": it's just too important an ally for you to ignore. ●

SO WHAT DO YOU NEED?
Your precise needs will clearly depend on the type of work you do, but these are bare essentials:

COMPUTER
Unless you're engaged in some *very* arcane business, a computer is a must.

TELECOMMUNICATIONS
If you want to speak to the outside world you need a telephone line. Most small businessmen are armed both with land lines and mobile phones. You also need at least one number where voice mails can be recorded – either on an answering machine or a message service provided by the phone company. Although e-mail has reduced the significance of faxes, they are still widely used, so it's a good idea either to have a fax machine (or software that can send and receive faxes). ●

TELEPHONE TALK

There was a time when any small business office would have required at least a couple of land lines: one for the telephone, one for fax, and, in recent years, one for the Internet. This issue is increasingly less clear cut these days. It's entirely possible for one man in an office equipped with a lap-top PC and a WAP mobile phone to communicate – talk and receive voice mail, send and receive faxes and e-mails, and browse the web – without any links to an external telephone line. For lap-tops with infra-red capabilities, no physical connection with the phone is even needed. So do you really need a land line at all?

In practice, mobile phones are still more expensive to use than fixed line systems, and they are also more expensive to call. Nonetheless, for most self-employed workers – especially those of the one-man-band variety – a mobile phone is an essential item.

This is a fast-developing and competitive area, so expect the costs of all types of telecommunication to fall in the future.

THE SECRETS OF SELF-EMPLOYMENT #17

There's no place for techofear! A computer and related telecoms technology are now facts of life. They are too important for any self-employed business person to ignore

CHOOSING A COMPUTER

This whole area is an anorak's dream. Ask one for his advice (it's always a "he") and you'll end up with a two-hour lecture. In truth, you can make this decision as simple or complicated as you like. On the one-hand you can pay a visit to one of the big "stack-em-up" computer warehouses and come out 30 minutes later with a complete set-up, or you can equally spend weeks scouring the computer press in search of the perfect system at the perfect price. Doubtless you will already know into which of those camps you naturally fall.

One thing that you do need to figure out up front, though, is the kinds of work you want to be able to do on your computer. For writing letters, hooking up to the Internet and doing spreadsheet calculations, the most modest of systems will be sufficient to meet your needs; for graphic design, heavy-duty image processing, dealing with audio and video more powerful systems are required.

COMPUTER BASICS

Let's take a look at the possibilities offered by a typical computer system. This should help to iron out confusion caused by some of the jargon that salesmen like to drop into conversation. Here are the two most basic buzzwords: HARDWARE and SOFTWARE. Hardware is everything "physical" about the machine – the parts you can see and feel. The software refers to the programs (or "applications") that make your computer work. Without software a computer is a useless piece of technology – it can't do a thing.

SPEED AND MEMORY

So how do you tell a good computer from a bad one? Easy – all computers are great! Some, though, deal with data much faster than others. This speed is governed by the machine's processing "chip", and is measured in megahertz (MHz). The best-known chips come from the Intel Pentium series.

You need to figure out up front what kinds of work you want to be able to do on your computer

The other major consideration you need to understand is that of data storage. This comes in two distinct forms: the hard disk, and random access memory (RAM). You can think of the hard disk as being your computer's filing cabinet. When you switch off the machine, the hard disk

THE SECRETS OF SELF-EMPLOYMENT #18
Size DOES matter – at least when you're talking about computers. Processors with higher MHz ratings will be faster, and drives with a higher Gigabyte value will store more data.

retains the information. RAM is different in that it is temporary storage: it only processes the data on which you are working at that moment. When you switch off, unless you have saved your work first, everything held in RAM will be lost.

It's fair to say that faster machines with greater storage capabilities are ALWAYS more desirable than their lesser counterparts. And unsurprisingly, the bigger and faster they are, the more they cost. It's really a matter of balancing your needs against your budget. ●

WHEREVER I LAY MY LAPTOP...

Of course, you don't necessarily have to have a bulky desktop computer system. Why not consider a portable, foldaway laptop? Until recently, there was no contest between standard desktop systems and laptops. Comparatively speaking, the latter were both costly and painfully slow. Although they are still invariably more expensive than similarly specified desk top machines, recent generations of Pentium 4 laptops and Macintosh G4 PowerBooks are extremely powerful beasts.

The only real drawback of using a laptop is the screen size. Although great for general writing and number crunching, those dealing with visual design are likely to find this a bit limiting. A laptop may not be an immediately obvious choice for everyone, but the flexibility this type of computer offers is well worth considering:

● **Portable**
● **Takes up no permanent desk space**
● **Ideal if you work on the move**
● **WAP technology allows you to connect to the Internet via a mobile phone.** ●

MAC VERSUS PC

Although there are plenty of different computers from which you can choose, they all fall into one of two camps: the PC and the Apple Macintosh. For some reason, discussing their relative merits can get people inexplicably hot under the collar. In truth, there is no simple answer. In terms of domestic market share, the PC is far more popular, although some industries are almost exclusively Mac-based.

In the past, Macs have been marketed as creative tools, allowing the user to get on with their business without having to worry about technology. Although that may be open to debate, they're certainly the "friendlier" of the two systems, and have a famously loyal following. Indeed, it's often said that Mac users swear by their machines whereas PC users are more likely to swear *at* theirs. And Macs look so much cooler.

One other consideration you might want to make, is that your system is compatible with those of your clients or suppliers. For most common applications this is not usually an issue, but for more specific tasks this may not be the case. Always check, anyway.

MAC BEATS PC

● Easier to use
● Harder to accidentally damage systems software
● Greater reputation for reliability
● Superior systems architecture
● Require less housekeeping maintenance – PCs easily get clogged up with system files

PC BEATS MAC

● Cheaper than Macs, and easily available on the high street.
● Usually packaged with freebies.
● Greater choice of programs (and PC software is invariably cheaper).

WHAT PARTS DO YOU NEED TO MAKE UP A COMPUTER?

When you're shopping for your first computer system, what exactly can you expect to get for your money? Whilst it's possible to build a PC pretty well from scratch, if you go into most high street computer stores you can expect to come out with a ready-to-use system.

THE BASIC KIT

Let's start with the "box". This is the system unit that houses the processing circuitry, hard disk, power supply and other elements of hardware. It will also contain the sockets into which all of the other pieces of hardware can be connected – these are the monitor screen, keyboard and mouse.

Most modern systems also come with a ready fitted modem (or "modulator/demodulator" if

WEB CONTACTS

www.apple.com	Apple Mac homepage
www.dell.com	PC systems
www.time.com	PC systems
www.sony.com	Sony PCs
www.epson.com	Printers
www.linotype-hell.com	Scanners
www.lacie.com	Disk drives
www.pace.com	Modems
www.usrobotics.com	Modems
www.hp.com	Various peripherals
www.iomega.com	Zip drives and cartridges
www.pcworld.co.uk	PC sales
www.macline.co.uk	Mac sales
www.intel.com	Processing chips
www.yamaha.com	CD drives

SAVE BEFORE IT'S TOO LATE

GET TO KNOW THE SAVE COMMAND: that's the first rule for those new to the world of computers. While you're working, get into the habit of saving every few minutes. If you're machine "crashes" (or siezes up) then your data loss should be minimal. Similarly, always make back-up copies of important documents away from your hard disk. DRIVES DON'T LAST FOREVER – if yours packs up, everything on it will be lost permanently.

you want to be formal about it). To connect to the Internet you must have a modem and subscribe to an Internet Service Provider.

PRINTERS AND SCANNERS

There are many other types of hardware that you can add to your system. If you're lucky you might get some of them bundled in with your basic kit.

If you want a paper version of the information on your screen you need either an inkjet or laser printer. Both can produce excellent results, although for the highest quality black and white output, laser is best; for colour printing, the inkjet is more practical, since the laser equivalent is still prohibitively expensive for most users (and the results may still not necessarily be that great.)

To put your own pictures on your computer you will need a scanner. You place your picture on a flat glass "bed" and the image is "read" line by line onto your hard disk. You can then alter the picture using a photo-manipulation program. Although scanners used to be terribly expensive, it's now possible to get one for under £100. Whilst this won't be good enough for professional use, it will be sufficient for creating images to use on a web site. Scanners can also turn printed words into computer text. To do this, an interpretation program is needed (these are sometimes bundled in with the scanner). Simply scan in the printed page and let the software do its magic.

EXTERNAL STORAGE

Finally, let's look at data storage away from the hard disk. Until recently, most computers came equipped only with floppy disk and CD drives. The traditional "floppy" can't hold very much data (around 1.3Mb) and is now approaching redundancy as a format. A popular alternative is the Iomega Zip cartridge, which is roughly the same size as a floppy but can hold at least 100Mb.

CD drives fitted to the most recent computers are capable of both reading and writing data. There are two types of CD: CD-R and CD-RW: data written to a CD-R can never be deleted; a CD-RW can be re-used many times. DVD drives can also be fitted, allowing you to watch films on your computer... if you really want to do that. ●

INSTALLING YOUR MACHINE

Back from the shops, once you've unpacked all your boxes, before you start putting everything together it's worth giving a little though to the positioning of your computer system.

First consider your surrounding environment. If your home office backs onto a kitchen or utility room, make sure there are no domestic appliances within a few metres the other side of a partition wall. The vibrations of washing machines are notorious for creating screen wobble which can, in the long run, cause damage to your monitor.

You should also put some thought into the height at which you set up your screen. Adrian Knowles of the Eye Care Information Service offers this advice: "On the desk, the screen itself should be positioned so you are looking slightly down on it, never directly at it or looking up... It's a question of sensible positioning of the computer. You usually know if you've got it wrong because you'll get adverse symptoms such as headaches."

STORAGE TERMS

All storage media are described in terms of how many "bytes" of data they hold. A byte is the memory needed to store a single character or number. Most hard disk drives are capable of storing BILLIONS of bytes. This is what those values actually mean:

Term	Abbreviations	Number of bytes
Kilobyte	K, KB	One Thousand
Megabyte	M, MB, "meg"	One Million
Gigabyte	G, GB, "gig"	One Billion
Terabyte	T, TB, "tera"	One Trillion

THE SECRETS OF SELF-EMPLOYMENT #19

Most computers are sold as a complete system including monitor, mouse, keyboard, modem and internal media drive. If you need a printer or scanner make sure you budget for these IN ADDITION to the cost of your basic system.

ESSENTIAL SOFTWARE

We've taken a look at hardware, now let's cast our eyes over the different types of program you can run on your computer. Once again, this is strictly beginners' stuff, so if you're computer-literate you might want to skip the next few pages.

TYPES OF PROGRAM

Once you've pressed the "on" button, to actually do anything useful on a computer you have to run a program (the "software"). When you type a letter, you run a program; when you perform calculations, you run a program; when you play a game, you run a program. You get the picture.

SOFTWARE PIRACY

Whether or not they like to think of it in such terms, most computer users at some point find themselves turning to crime – by using illegal software. Whilst we all like the idea of getting something for nothing, the fact of the matter is that using pirated software is theft. Would you walk into a computer store and shoplift a computer game? In the eyes of the law, using "bootleg" software amounts to much the same thing. Although it's widely viewed as a petty "non-crime" – like taking pencils from the company stationery cupboard – and the likelihood of prosecution is very slight, it nonetheless costs the likes of Microsoft millions of dollars in lost revenue every year. Whilst Bill Gates and his buddies can afford this annoyance, new generations of young innovators are certain to be less financially resiliant. So it's not only against the law, but it helps to suppress progress and competition. Although nearly everybody does it, it isn't a practice we should encourage.

Programs have been devised to perform all manner of tasks. Here are some of the types of program you might find useful:

- **Word Processing**
- **Spreadsheets and accounts**
- **Desktop publishing**
- **E-mail and browsing the web**
- **Games**
- **Graphic design**
- **Digital photography and image manipulation**
- **Diary systems**
- **Listening to music**
- **Recording and editing sound and video**
- **Digital photography.**

OPERATING SYSTEMS

Before we go any further, let's give a brief mention to a critical, but largely transparent, piece of software – the operating system. This doesn't do anything particularly interesting in its own right, but takes care of the way in which your computer runs its programs and organises data. It also allows you to personalise aspects of its operation, such as the visual appearance of data on the screen.

There are two widely used operating systems. Nearly all PCs run a version of Microsoft Windows: 2000 Professional, 98 or 95. Apple Macintoshes have their own operating system called MAC OS: the most current version is System X, although 8 and 9 are both commonly found on many machines.

A newer (and reputedly superior) system, Linux currently has a small number of users, although its popularity is growing. Versions of it can be run on both PC and Mac. ●

WORD PROCESSING

Less than 20 years ago, if you wanted to produce a letter that was not hand-written then you had to have a typewriter. Until, almost overnight, the home computer revolution rendered it an obsolete piece of technology.

For most self-employed persons, familiarity with word processing software is essential. Word processors are equipped with some handy features:

- **Type letters and brochures**
- **Edit and reformat text after it has been entered on screen**
- **Alter the fonts, type size and style**
- **Create templates for letters and mailshots.**

The most popular word processor is Microsoft Word. Recent versions allow you not only to input

PROGRAM COMPATIBILITY

In theory, text generated by any word processor can be read by any *other* word processing program on any type of computer. This is because all such software can read "plain text". However, each program has its own methods of dealing with format instructions — these are details such as margins, tabs, line spacing and justification. This means that documents saved in the Microsoft Word format may not necessarily be interpreted by the Claris Works program (or, indeed, by different versions of Microsoft Word). Compatibility can only be guaranteed when documents are SAVED as plain text.

and edit text, but create design layouts, draw pictures and add photographs. Other widely used software includes Claris Works and WordPerfect. They all do the job in hand equally well. ●

Microsoft Word: position the cursor on the screen using the mouse and start typing.

SPREADSHEETS

If you want to perform basic number-crunching operations on your computer, spreadsheet software such as Microsoft Excel or Lotus 1-2-3 can provide you with an excellent flexible solution:

- **Can handle the simplest arithmetic to complex mathematical equations**
- **Ideal for bookkeeping**
- **Can be used as a simple database, for example, to hold customer details**
- **Can use on-screen data to create charts and graphs.**

HOW DO SPREADSHEETS WORK?

The concept is devilishly simple. The screen contains a matrix of "cells" which can be uniquely referred by row and column. Each row is given a number; each column a letter – in the example below, cell B6 contains the number 198762.99.

Each of these cells may contain either text, numbers or a mathematical formula. The calculations are performed by referring to the

numerical data in other cells. If you look at cell B14 in the first example (*bottom left*) you will see that it contains the words "SUM(B2:B13)". This is an instruction to add up all of the values between cells B2 and B13. In the second example (*bottom right*), you can see how the contents of cell B14 has been updated to display that total. If any of the values in the cells above are altered, the figure in cell B14 will change accordingly. This clearly makes spreadsheets ideal for bookkeeping.

It's easy to get impressive results quickly using a spreadsheet, although getting to grips with the more complex features will take a good deal of time. ●

Microsoft Excel spreadsheet

You can produce professional-looking presentations using Microsoft PowerPoint software.

PRESENTATIONS

From time to time, your work may require you to give formal presentations. Specialised software such as Microsoft PowerPoint can help you to organise and create professional presentations:

- **Create and design your own slide shows**
- **Connect your computer to a screen projector to give fully automated multimedia presentations**
- **Provide printed copy for your audience**
- **Automatically create web pages from your presentation.** ●

THE FULL SET

You can get budget versions of Word, Excel and PowerPoint (as well as Internet software) bundled together as a part of the Microsoft Office range. This is an economical way of buying software.

VIRUSES: BEWARE!

Usually distributed across the Internet, a virus is a tiny program specifically designed to do harm. The perpetrators usually seem to be very bright teenage nerdy types who can't get girlfriends and so take out their frustrations on the rest of the world. Although most of the viruses that get unleashed are relatively benign, if you get landed with one, at worst, your hard disk could suffer irreparable data corruption. Yet another good reason to make back-up copies of data.

The growth of this nuisance now means that it is becoming increasingly important for every computer to be kitted out with some kind of "anti-virus" program. The principle is simple – each time you download data from the Internet (or from any other external source, such as a floppy disk, CD-ROM or Zip cartridge) it will be vetted by the program for known viruses. The software can also be used to "vaccinate" for existing viruses. It's a bit sad that we have to take such steps, but it's better to safe than sorry.

THE SECRETS OF SELF-EMPLOYMENT #20

The vast majority of web traffic comes from search engines. Before you create any web pages, read up on what you need to do to register your site with them

the internet

If you connect two or more computers you have what is called a "network". The Internet is the greatest network of them all, quite literally linking together millions of computers across the world, allowing their owners to exchange information.

IT SEEMS LIKE no time has passed since the Internet was *the* great new buzzword, and phrases like "information superhighway" and "surfing in cyberspace" were being bandied across the media. For those of us who jumped in right at the start, these terms now sound like quaint hipster slang from a bygone period. The Internet has inveigled itself into everyday life so effectively that many of us take for granted the idea of communicating with friends in Australia every day, buying CDs from an American website, or reading the on-line version of the *New York Times* with our morning coffee.

But this actually describes reality for a fairly small proportion of the population. In truth, the Internet still worries or baffles a lot of people for whom it could provide untold benefits.

THE GLOBAL ONE-MAN BAND

More than any other single factor, the possibilities opened up by the rapid spread of the Internet has influenced the growth of self-employment as a viable alternative to everyday corporate life. This is especially true for those that management guru Peter Drucker anointed "knowledge workers". Armed with just a laptop, a modem and a phone line, those with suitable skills are able to operate successfully in a global environment from the comfort of their own home.

The Internet is likely to play a significant role in your working life

GOOD FOR BUSINESS

However you view the Internet, one way or another it's likely to play a significant role in your life as a self-employed operator. Not only does it allow communication directly with your customers, associates, clients and potential clients, but it provides access to an uncharted repository of information held on "servers" all over the world. Furthermore, by creating a presence on the World Wide Web, you can advertise and sell your products or services anywhere in the world… well, at least to anyone who is connected to the Internet. ●

MAIN FUNCTIONS

Here is a brief look at the Internet activities likely to be of most use to small businesses or self-employed workers.

E-MAIL

This is a basic necessity. You type a message into your computer, connect to the Internet and press a button. In theory, your message should arrive at its destination anywhere in the world within a few minutes. And all for the cost of a quick local telephone call. The most popular e-mail programs are Qualcomm's Eudora, Claris Mailer and Microsoft Outlook. You can also send and receive mail using a web browser (see below).

WORLD WIDE WEB

Using web browsers such as Microsoft Internet Express or Netscape Communicator, you can view any websites set up anywhere in the world. If you want to sell or advertise your own services or products you need to get "homepage" set up. At the moment, around 25% of Britain's self-employed have their own web space. But this number is sure to rise rapidly.

NEWSGROUPS

A newsgroup (or "Usenet" group) is rather like a public notice board on which messages can be posted, read and answered. There are tens of thousands of different newsgroups on the Internet, many of which cover VERY specific subjects. Newsgroups are really useful for solving problems. When you find the right newsgroup all you do is post your query – someone out there is sure to have an answer of some sort.

Although specific newsgroup software does exist, most people either use their web browser or e-mail program. ●

WEB CONTACTS

Who says there's no such thing as a free lunch? One of the great things about the Internet is that much of the software you need to carry out the functions shown on this page can be acquired at no cost. One good source is the free CD-ROMs that usually come free with monthly Internet magazines. Alternatively, they can be downloaded from the Internet. Here are some useful web addresses for free software:

www.microsoft.com	Outlook Express (mail)
	Internet Explorer (web)
www.netscape.com	Communicator (web)
www.eudora.com	Eudora (mail)
www.pegasus.usa.com	
	Pegasus (mail)
www.freeware.com	Free software directory
www.freewarehome.com	
www.shareware.com	Try-before-you-buy software directory
www.download.cnet.com	
	Massive archive of free software

75% of Britain's self-employed use e-mail for work – compared to 16% of the public as a whole

Alodis/MORI poll, 2000

GETTING CONNECTED

Most Internet software is easy to use. For many novices, the tough bit is getting connected in the first place – and even that's fairly straightforward these days. Before you can do anything, though, you need to find an ISP – an Internet Service Provider. This is a company that hires (or "gives") you dial-in access to the Internet. There are an incredible number of ISPs currently operating in the UK. Some of them charge a small monthly fee; others are "free". The latter term needs some qualification, since although there is no connection fee, they often recoup their costs through telephone charges for using their support lines.

FILE TRANSFER AND SPEED

For many small businesses, the Internet can reduce costs dramatically by allowing conventional post to be sidelined. Where large amounts of data have to be transferred from one destination to another, files of less that a couple of megabytes in size can be sent as "attachments" to regular e-mail transmissions.

The precise speed at which data is sent and received is determined by the limitations of your modem and telephone line. The standard modem speed is 56K (56,000 bits per second), which with most phone lines translates to a rate of between 40-45K.

Faster Internet access times (up to 500K) can be achieved by leasing "broadband" ADSL connections, although at this time, costs are at least 5 times that of standard access. If you need to send very large amounts of data, an ISDN line will provide the best results. Neither the ADSL and ISDN systems use standard modems – both require the purchase of specialised hardware and software.

It's not that easy to judge how good or reliable an ISP will be. Although some Internet magazines publish technical performance data it's probably fair to say that the vast majority are much of muchness. If in doubt, canvas opinion from friends and colleagues – bad reputations usually precede dodgy operators.

INTERNET PROTOCOLS

When you register, your ISP will give you a phone number, a user ID and a password. Assuming that you have a modem connected to a phone line, when this data is correctly entered into your computer, you can automatically dial-in for Internet access. This is enough to get you hooked up to the World Wide Web.

E-MAIL CONNECTIONS

To send and receive e-mails there is some extra information you need. Don't worry, all of this will be given to you by your ISP, and must then be entered into your e-mail software:

● **Your e-mail address**
● **Your ISP's outgoing mail server (usually the SMTP server)**
● **Your ISP's incoming mail server (usually the POP3 server)**
● **Your POP3 ID**
● **Your POP3 password.**

AUTOMATIC SET UP

If that all sounds a bit long-winded, some ISPs provide a CD-Rom that, when run, automatically sets up the necessary configurations. You click the start button and respond to question prompts. When you've finished, you're ready to roll. ●

THE SECRETS OF SELF-EMPLOYMENT #21

"Real brands don't emerge from theories – they are made by real people who have a passion for something" – the Brand Guardians website

CREATING A DOMAIN

When you register with a service provider, your choice of e-mail address and web URL will be compromised by having to include the ISP's name. If your business is called AUDIOPHONIX and you register with an ISP called FREECONNECT, then your e-mail address may be fsmith@audiophonix.freeconnect.co.uk. How much more professional would that look if you could lose the name of the ISP? You can do this by using a specialist domain hosting company.

You first need to find out if your desired name is available – you can do this by logging onto the domain host's website and performing a search. Costs depend on the services provided, but a fee of under £20 a year ought to get you a simple forwarding service. In the example above, that would mean that any e-mail sent to fsmith@audiophonix.com would instantly pass to the existing "Freeconnect" address: nobody need know that it's a free ISP rather than run an impressive leased line system. It would also mean that anyone entering the URL www.audiophonix.com could connect directly to the "free" web address.

YOUR OWN WEB PAGE

As we have seen from the proliferation of failed "dot.com" enterprises, basing a business on the Internet can be risky. There's no question, though, that most of us can benefit from some form of presence on the World Wide Web.

A simple homepage can act as permanent mail-shot, able to show anyone who logs onto your web address the range of your activities. Indeed, many self-employed professionals upload what amounts to an on-line CV. After all, you never know who'll be browsing. Some go further, selling their wares directly to customers. If you manufacture your products this has clear advantages in that you reap the full retail price rather than having to sell at wholesale prices to other outlets. But there are risks attached: surveys still indicate a degree of consumer mistrust of buying from the Internet.

Most of us can benefit from some sort of presence on the Web

Although anyone with a few brain cells can put together a simple but effective homepage using free web software, the skills and effort needed to create a sophisticated secure credit card system are somewhat greater – leave that to the professionals.

Always remember, your website is your shop window. If it doesn't work or looks amateurish, why should anyone think that your services are likely to be any different. **A POOR WEBSITE IS WORSE THAN NO WEBSITE AT ALL.** ●

me
unltd

4

in this chapter...

your brand is your business

The most exhilarating aspect of self-employment is that success or failure rides on a single person – YOU. Although some people might find such responsibility a heavy burden, the most effective independent workers relish the fact that they can apply their own unique brand values to their field of work.

WE LIVE IN AN ERA where branding is not only a business essential, it's just about unavoidable. Everywhere we look in any large town in just about any country in the world we find ourselves surrounded by familiar symbols: the Macdonald "arches", the Nike "swoosh". They're relentless. There is no escape.

The art of branding is all about focus and communication. And emotional reaction. The most successful brands have created a new language – a kind of shorthand that can sum up immediately with a single logo or trademarked phrase a set of core values. The psychology of branding is to provide the consumers, customer or client with a sure-fire emotional trigger.

The most successful brands are able to use a phrase or logo to sum up a set of core values

Think of the phrase "It's The Real Thing". Unless you've been living a peculiarly isolated existence for the past 30 years, at the very least, two words will come straight to mind – **Coca Cola**. It will probably also conjure up a mental image of the classic logo wrapped around that uniquely shaped glass bottle. That's all well and good, but what the brand creators *really* want is an emotional response. When you hear that phrase, they want you to think long hot summers, lazy days lounging in the park, good times shared with friends. We're not talking about the ultimate in feel-good narcotics here, but a bottle of brown, caffeinated, sugary, fizzy pop. It's faintly ludicrous, isn't it? And yet it clearly works. ●

THE "ME" BRAND

It's clear that the basic corporate business models for marketing and selling products can also be used for single-player businesses. Your ideal should be to create a "brand" for yourself that sparks off the same kind of emotional associations in the minds of your clients or customers. So how can you come up with your own effective brand? Start with this simple test:

● Ask yourself this question: **WHAT IS IT ABOUT WHAT I'M DOING THAT SETS ME APART FROM OTHERS?**

● Now try to answer that question **IN LESS THAN 20 WORDS** (remember, were trying to come up some pithy soundbites here).

● Read your answer several times over. Now read it back out loud. How does it sound? Does it impress you? Or more to the point, do you think it would it register with a prospective client? Or get nodding approval from existing satisfied clients?

If that exercise leaves you in any doubt, then you need to put serious thought into developing yourself as a brand. This is not a afterthought. It should strike at the very heart of your business, irrespective of its nature.

> ❝ You're every bit as much a brand as Nike, Coke, Pepsi and the Body Shop. To start thinking like your own brand manager, ask yourself the same same questions as the brand managers at Nike, Coke, Pepsi and the Body Shop ask themselves. What is it that my product or service does that makes it different? ❞
>
> **Tom Peters,** *corporate branding expert*

> ## THE SECRETS OF SELF-EMPLOYMENT #22
>
> "The key to any personal branding is word-of-mouth marketing... so the big trick to building your brand is to find ways to nurture your network of colleagues" – Tom Peters.

Concentrate on those differences – they're critical, As Swedish economists Jonas Ridderstråle and Kjell Nordström conclude in their seminal book, *Funky Business,* "The average never wins... to succeed we must stop being so goddam normal. If we behave like all the others, we will see the same things, come up with similar ideas, and develop identical products and services." ●

CORE VALUES

Complementing this differentiation is the creation of an identifiable set of values. This means looking a little deeper into what your business is *really* going to be all about. Coca Cola is NOT all about selling fizzy drink – anyone can do that. It IS about fluffier notions like the joy and togetherness that the product can bring. All brands have a set of values. And yours will be no different. They describe the things that are important to YOU, and also provide a benchmark with which you are able to measure success. ➜

DEFINING THOSE VALUES

To identify your own core values, you need to come up with a small number (no more than a half a dozen) of adjectives that describe the way you want your business to be perceived.

Friendly	Dynamic	Conservative
Cutting-edge	Efficient	Imaginative
Thoughtful	Courteous	Reliable
Energetic	Purposeful	Cheap
Fast	Thorough	Safe
Creative	Evangelical	Entertaining

Those are all possibilities you could consider – there are obviously many others. The critical point, though, is that once you have built that set of core values, they sit above everything your business does. Every decision you take can be measured against those values. Brands are nothing if not consistent or else they wouldn't be able to invoke those same emotional responses time and time again. That's why Coke adverts feature happy smiling faces, NOT brightly coloured cutting-edge graphics backed by loud dance music: these do not represent Coke values. ●

WEB CONTACTS

The following sites provide further useful information on the subject of branding:

www.brandguardians.com

www.myprimetime.com

www.tompeters.com

www.faithpopcorn.com

For a provocative read on the power of branding take a look at *No Logo* by Naomi Klein.

DO YOU NEED A BRAND NAME?

You already have one – your parents thought it up years ago. If you work independently it isn't always necessary to come up with a new identity, even if it may make creating a brand "personality" easier. This of course depends on the nature of your business. The advantage of using your own name is that your contacts already know it. If you go down this route, you should consider registering your name as a company, trademark (*see right*) or an Internet domain (*see page 91*). Of course, one rather obvious downside is that unless you have a highly unusual name, it's unlikely to be unique.

SHOULD I DESIGN MY OWN STATIONERY?

Design is a bit like singing – everybody thinks they can do it. The proliferation of cheap, easy-to-use desktop design programs have meant that those with a bit of visual flair can get polished-looking results. The problem with many first-time designers is that they fail to understand the "less is more" law. If there are two things guaranteed to mark out an amateur design, they are the overuse of colour and a multiplicity of typefaces. Sloppy, half-baked or amateurish business stationery can carry a significant implication – not least if you don't appear to care enough to get your branded persona right, then maybe your work will be similarly poor.

If you design your own stationery, keep it simple. Otherwise hand it over to a professional designer.

For new names, try to make them distinctive, memorable and reflect your brand values. A strap line slogan can be useful to reinforce the strength of your brand. Here's how to create one:

● **Write a brief description of what you do**
● **Now make it shorter**
● **Now make it shorter still.**

For a brand strap-line to work it should be no more than eight words long - look at classics such as BT's "It's Good To Talk".

NO LOGO?

All the great brands have a strong visual identity. But is it really necessary for, say, an independent accountant to have a logo? No, of course not - in some cases it could even be viewed as a little pretentious. Careful use of colour and typography in your business stationery can be used to create a distinctive and professional look. ●

THE SECRETS OF SELF-EMPLOYMENT #23

Always start with a hook. This should be a single paragraph that outlines in brief the benefits you can provide. Don't forget, many busy executives won't bother to look at a document that doesn't have a management summary.

TRADEMARKS

A trade mark is used to distinguish the products of one trader from those of another. It can take the form of words, logos, pictures, or a combination of all three. A good trade mark is instantly recognisable – think of the famous Nike "swoosh".

Trade marks in the UK are the responsibility of the Patent Office.

Before you can register your trade mark, ensure that if fulfils the legal criteria:

● Distinctive for the goods/services on offer
● Not deceptive, or contrary to law or morality
● Not the same as any previously registered marks for the same or similar goods/services
● Not based around words or phrases that could be applied to any other business: "24-HOURS A DAY", for example, would be disallowed. (Quirky or alternative spelling won't fix the problem, either: "24 HOURZ A DAY" still wouldn't get registered).

It costs £200 to apply for a trade mark. This is an non-returnable fee – you pay even if your application is rejected – so make sure that similar trade marks have not already been registered. (*see below*).

Applying for a trade mark is simple – you fill out a *TM3* document. This can be downloaded in "pdf" form or requested by calling the Central Enquiry Unit (08459 500 505). The Patent Office should examine your application within two months of receipt. It will either be accepted or you'll receive a report detailing objections.

A really useful guide to the whole issue of trade marks can also be downloaded from the Patent Office's website (**www.patent.gov.uk/tm**).

SELLING YOURSELF

"If a man write a better book, preach a better sermon, or make a better mousetrap than his neighbour, though he build his house in the woods, the world will make a beaten path to his door."

Ralph Waldo Emerson (1803-1882)

Things must have been very different in the 19th century, because – wise man that he was – the oft-quoted Mr Emerson couldn't have got the basic principles of business any more wrong. The only reason the world will buy that "better mousetrap" is if they are first told of its existence. And then exactly why it's better than the competition, how much it costs, and finally where it can be bought.

To carry out this marketing process effectively requires the development of skills as a salesman. If you are an independent operator that means that

no matter how great your product or service, you will at some point also have to turn your hand to selling yourself.

Some people are natural salesmen. For them, the adrenaline rush of chasing and winning new business is one of the thrills of the job. Others find it so daunting that they can become physically sick. But even if you are not the original Mr Charisma, there are plenty of steps you can take to make a successful sales pitch. Before any of this, though, you need first to target your clients.

WHO WILL BUY?

Finding an approach to identifying customers or clients will obviously differ depending on whether you're selling a product to the general public or offering a professional service to a client. However, the general principles remain much the same. However, before you can hope to succeed in any business, you need to gain a firm understanding of the way your specific market works.

> **Before you can hope to succeed in any business, you need an understanding of the way your market works**

MARKET RESEARCH

However limited your initial resources, you will have to engage in some form of market research. A good first port of call is your local reference library. In its commercial section you should find trade directories and publications relating to your area of activity; *Yellow Pages* phone books covering the entire country; directories of foreign importers, and much more besides. If you want data relating to your trade or industry, the

> **❝** My first record release was a complete disaster. I was so convinced it would be a hit that I pressed up 5,000 copies just for starters. A year later, four-and-a-half thousand of them were still in my Dad's garage! I didn't get advance feedback from a distributor... to be honest, I hadn't even started looking for a distributor! What was I thinking, that fans would be hammering on my door with £5 notes in their hands? **❞**
>
> **Tom Francke,** *record label owner*

government's Office for National Statistics (ONS) has vast amounts of information that you can access on demand (**www.ons.gov.uk**). The more you understand about the way your market works, the easier it will be to get your sales pitch hitting the right targets.

MAIL SHOTS

Your initial market research should aim to create a list of organisations that you hope to be able to turn into future clients. Get as much detailed information as you can. ALWAYS TRY TO GET A CONTACT NAME RATHER THAN A JOB TITLE – it only takes a quick phone call and will help to make your initial approach as personal as possible.

A mail shot is not that far removed from a press release (we'll cover these in detail on page 101). It should aim to give your client a brief overview of what you have to offer:

● **Use no more than a single page of headed notepaper. The idea is to whet the appetite not tell your life story**
● **Introduce your reason for writing in a brief pithy paragraph**
● **Give a bullet-pointed list of the services you can provide**
● **Wherever possible, highlight reasons why your services are different from (or better than) your competitors.**

THE DIRECT APPROACH

If you're really bold – and this isn't recommended for the weak-hearted – you could pick up the phone and make a direct approach. If you manage to get past the personal assistant without the

PAPER OR E-MAIL?

The trouble with mail shots is that they are expensive and have a low hit rate. For every 50 you send out, you'll be doing well to get a single positive response. And it will have cost you £13.50 in postage alone.

So how about creating an electronic mailing list? Sending an e-mail is certainly cheaper. The problem is that it's hard to get your brand persona across in an e-mail – all the prospective client sees is raw text. A good alternative is to set up a web page containing the full graphic mailshot. You then hardwire the URL (the web page address) into the e-mail. This gives the client the choice of viewing your web page if more information is required.

phone being slammed down, introduce yourself, discuss the reason you are calling VERY briefly, and request a meeting in person. Make sure that you take up as little time as possible. In truth, this is a risky gambit – many people don't like to feel they are being hassled. ●

THE SECRETS OF SELF-EMPLOYMENT #24
The average business person has an attention span of six minutes – *Business Week*.

ADVERTISING AND PR

If your product or service is aimed at the general public rather other companies, you'll initially have to engage in some form of advertising. If your business is based on reaching a local market, begin by making a list of the local media available, including newspapers and magazines, local radio and television.

> **"** I was sceptical about advertising my services. I could see that if you had a product to sell that it was unavoidable, but as an accountant I wasn't sure how it could work. My wife talked me into to it, suggesting that I should target particular industries and place adverts in their trade newspapers. I spent around £250 for three boxes. I got 17 responses and 4 new clients as a result. It seems so obvious now, but it didn't then. **"**
>
> **Thomas Greville, *certified accountant***

WHICH MEDIA TO USE

Your aim is to reach the largest possible number of potential customers. And to spend as little as possible in achieving that aim. Clearly, choosing the right place to advertise is going to be a critical decision. When considering a newspaper, magazine or other media, start by asking yourself these questions:

Dividing the advertising fees by the circulation tells you the cost per reader

- **Are you sure that it is read, watched or listened to by your potential customer?**
- **What is the circulation or coverage?**
- **What is the cost of advertising?**

Finding true circulation figures can be tricky. Many of the larger national magazines have their sales figures audited by the Audit Bureau of Circulations (ABC), but elsewhere you'll have to rely on the honesty of the publisher or broadcasters' advertising sales teams.

It goes without saying that you want your advertising to be as cost-effective as possible. One way of deciding which media to use is to take the quoted cost of the advert and divide it by the circulation. The result is a cost-per-reader figure. This is obviously a crude measurement since it assumes that all of the circulations have an equally relevant mix of potential customers, but it will give you a feel for getting the best value for money.

POSITIONING YOUR ADVERT

The cost of a magazine advert will also depend on its size and position in the journal. The cheapest ones will appear in the "classifieds" at the back of the magazine. These only work if a customer is actively looking for a specific product or service. They won't be eye-catching enough to grab the casual reader. There are no hard-and-fast rules about optimum positioning, but advertising industry wisdom suggests that these four points are worth following:

- **In the first quarter or third of the magazine**
- **On a news or editorial page**
- **On a right-hand page**
- **One third the size of a page.**

CONTENT

It can be tempting to overcomplicate your advert. So when discussing content never lose sight of the basic essence of your message.

- **Have a clear, unambiguous, straightforward message**
- **A sparse look featuring plenty of white background space usually works best**
- **Use as few words as you can – the less work the reader has to do the better**
- **Take care with using humour or very stylised design – you don't want to alienate potential customers just because they may have different tastes from you**
- **The main thrust of an advert should ALWAYS concentrate on the benefits of buying your product or service, rather than focussing on you yourself.**

Although many small businesses do the copy, design and layout for themselves, if you want a professional look, think about hiring a freelance designer or the services of a small advertising agency. Some magazines and newspapers can offer their own design service at an extra cost.

FREQUENCY

Advertising at this basic level is a gradual process. Placing a single advert that runs for one week or one month is, in all honesty, next to useless. A series of adverts well placed over a period of time will help to build up a general awareness of your business. It should both act as a reminder to existing customers, and – ideally – lodge your name in the minds of anyone who might need your services in the future. ●

WRITING A PRESS RELEASE

A press release is a great way to get free publicity. The aim is to get news about your activities to the market place in the form of news articles or stories. Indeed, the public relations function is an important adjunct to advertising in that information is presented to the public by journalists rather than the business itself, therefore it has more objective credibility.

Here are some simple guidelines to help you create the perfect press release:

Presentation

- Make it clear that it is a press release. Write "PRESS RELEASE" at the top of the page.
- Add your own name or your trading name.
- Give your press release a date and number
- Give your contact details
- Keep it short – one page is the ideal
- Give it a catchy, meaningful title
- A well-presented press release reflects well on its sender: poor examples usually find their way on to the newsroom's "wall-of-shame" noticeboard

Three-paragraph system

- **Paragraph 1** tells the basic story – the who, what, when, where and why
- **Paragraph 2** should be a quote that backs up paragraph 1. A quote gives a press release credibility... even if you are the source of the quote
- **Paragraph 3** explains who you are and what you do

And finally...

- Keep your sentences short, the page uncluttered and written in a sensible type face.
- Make sure that the facts are accurate.
- Make sure it's addressed to the right target.
- Make yourself available for further comment after you send your press release.

THE BIG PITCH

So, you've got a foot in the door. A potential client has expressed an interest in what you have to offer. Now is your chance to *really* impress.

KNOW ABOUT YOUR AUDIENCE

Like public speaking (*see pages 104-105*), the key to making a good sales pitch is down to preparation. That can involve a degree of detective work. Find out as much as you can about the company, its culture, performance and approach to business. If you can get a handle on the kind of people who work there, you'll have a better chance of setting the tone of your pitch at the right level. Trying to impress a roomful of merchant bankers will require a different presentation and vernacular than pitching to a group of press officers. Giving the same presentation to every potential client is a guaranteed loser (not to mention being really boring). All clients are different and all of them merit a fresh approach.

Use your imagination when building this company profile. You can get often get a feel for the attitude a company presents to the world by reading features in trade magazines. Ring up their PR department and ask for literature. Visit their website. Root around – see if anyone you know has direct experience of working with that client.

> **❝** Researching your audience is vital. A technique that impresses one client with our creativity could be a mere gimmick to another.**❞**
> **Tina Brown, *Outside The Box***

NO STONE UNTURNED...

YOU CAN'T BE TOO PREPARED. This point can't be rammed home enough. As soon has you been invited to present your case, try to talk to the person who organised the meeting. Find out how much time you will have for your pitch, how many people will be attending (and their positions in the company), what the environment is like and what visual aids are available. The last thing you need is to turn up having spent days preparing a sophisticated computer-based presentation, only to find that there's no projector or screen. This probably won't endear you to the client.

WHAT DO YOU WANT TO HAPPEN NEXT?

Go into your meeting or presentation with an agenda. Ask yourself what you want to get out of the meeting, and gear your pitch around this. Your approach at this stage may still be speculative, in which case your main aim should be to create an impression for future reference. When preparing your presentation, keep in mind these four factors:

- **It can be tempting to gear a pitch towards what you want to give, rather than what the client actually needs. Avoid this approach**
- **Focus less on the actual features of your product or service than on the benefits that it can bring to the client**
- **Keep it real. Only discuss features and benefits that are relevant to the client, or the job in hand**
- **Keep it brief. Assume the client is always VERY busy, and so ensure that you can summarise what you have to offer in no more than 10 minutes.**

THE SECRETS OF SELF-EMPLOYMENT #25

"If you forget water and dry up, bite the side of your tongue to get the saliva flowing" – Mary Spillane, *Branding Yourself.*

> **"**I get annoyed when people don't understand the power of silence and keep rattling on. When somebody is presenting their ideas I need time to think, to consider what they are offering and whether it fits with our plans. I have a great respect for people who know when to shut up and who can deal comfortably with silence rather than starting to panic.**"**
>
> **Martin Lashwood, *interactive editor, Xebec***

gives the impression that your response requires a moment's thought. If you don't know the answer to a question, it's probably best to admit it than respond with a load of waffly nonsense off the top of your head.

To really build a strong relationship with your audience you need to call on all your non-verbal communication skills. Make eye contact with everyone in the room, although avoid focusing your attention on the person you believe holds the most authority.

THE BIG MOMENT

Everyone is gathered to hear you talk, but before you begin, find out each attending person's role within the company. This will enable you to direct information toward the relevant personnel.

Addressing an audience can be a nerve-racking experience (*see pages 104-105 for practical guidance*), but if you can make the flow of information a two-way thing, you're unlikely to feel as self-conscious. This means listening as well as talking. With that in mind, take care that you don't speed through your presentation. Pacing is one of the great arts of oratory – nothing betrays a speaker's lack of confidence more than talking too quickly. Give your audience time to absorb what you are saying. They also might want to ask questions. If they do, take a few moments of silence before giving your answer. It

THE POST-MORTEM

Although you're unlikely to hear immediately whether or not your pitch was successful, try not to show too strong an emotion either way at the end of the meeting – appearing to be arrogant (or desperate) won't do your cause any good in the future.

Avoid subconsciously (or otherwise) addressing your pitch to the person you believe holds the purse strings

A few days after the presentation, write a brief note of thanks to the client, summarising very briefly once again what you have to offer. You never know, it might just sway a split decision. ●

SPEAKING IN PUBLIC

It's a universal *bête noir*. Stop any number of people in any high street in any country and ask them to name their greatest dreads – public speaking will be high on many of those lists. Being nervous about "performing" before an audience is natural, but there are steps you can take to help manage anxiety and ensure cool and confident presentations.

KNOW YOUR MATERIAL

When presentations go pear-shaped, it's usually because the material hasn't been learned well enough. This is a basic necessity. Actors are taught that they must commit their lines so deeply to memory that recall is automatic. Only when you've done this can the real business of performing begin. THIS MEANS ENDLESS REHEARSAL.

Once you know your script, do as many dry runs as you can, preferably in front of a small audience. Ask them for their views: Did it flow smoothly? Was the pacing right? Was it dull? Don't be put off by criticism – think of it as an opportunity to hone your material and performance.

Try to recreate as closely as possible the scene of the eventual presentation. If you can rehearse in the same room then so much the better. The more familiar you are with your surroundings, material and props, the more your confidence will grow.

DEALING WITH NERVES

No matter how experienced they may be, the best performers ALWAYS suffer nerves before an event. Not only is this normal, it's desirable: it shows that they care enough to want to give the best to their audience. TOO MUCH nervous energy, though, can destabilise a performance. Seasoned orators have their own routines for releasing excess energy. The trick is to let out just enough to calm anxieties, but without creating an undesirably stress-free state. Calisthenic exercise, such as running on the spot, gently shaking your arms and legs, or laying into a punch bag, are popular techniques. On a gentler note, yoga or breathing exercises can relieve tension:

- **Close your eyes and clear your lungs**
- **Inhale very slowly through the nose**
- **Hold your breath for ten seconds**
- **Exhale quickly through the mouth**
- **Repeat at least ten times.**

NEVER APOLOGISE

How many times have you heard a presentation begin with the speaker proclaiming his or her nerves? This is ALWAYS a bad idea. Don't forget, most of your audience are also scared of public speaking. This merely takes their focus away from your message and places it firmly on YOU. It's often said that audiences can smell fear. That may be true, but usually they don't *want* to; it puts them on edge. If they are not comfortable, your message has even less chance of getting through.

> **❝** I became an excellent public speaker because rather than once a week, I booked myself to speak *three times a day* to anyone who would listen. While others in my organisation had forty-eight speaking engagements a year, I would have a similar number within *two weeks*. **❞**
> **Anthony Robbins, *motivational guru***

Although easier said than done, if you find yourself overcome with anxiety during your speech, try not to panic. Stop. Collect your thoughts. Breathe in deeply. Take a sip of water. Resume. Again, this may "worry" your audience, so it's a good idea to lighten the atmosphere with a humourous aside. (Perhaps one that you prepared earlier.)

THE MORE YOU DO...

It's hardly surprising that so many people think of themselves as being hopeless public speakers. Outside of the "performance" professions how often do most of us face an audience? Hardly ever. The fact of the matter is that few people get to be good at *anything* without practical experience. The more speeches you give, the better you will be. And that's a guarantee.

Most adult education centres offer courses in public communications. You may not learn too much more new information than is shown here, but the real value comes in enabling you to put theory into practice. Lessons usually end with each student giving a brief talk before the class. If you attend one night a week for 12 weeks, by the end the course you will have done more formal public speaking than most people manage in a lifetime.

DON'T BE INTIMIDATED

The audience is on your side. They want to informed, stimulated and entertained. Why would they want you to fail? Even if your oratory skills are only modest, if you are properly prepared and well-rehearsed, you will be able to give an effective speech. ●

THE SECRETS OF SELF-EMPLOYMENT #26

If you give great advice, you get a reputation. Occasionally someone will rip you off or take advantage of you, but that is far outweighed by the loyalty you create" – Simon Woodroffe, in interview with *Alodis* magazine.

THE OLD UNDERPANTS TRICK

Let's lay this old chestnut to rest. To overcome fear, the anxious speaker visualises his entire audience in an equally anxious state – the classic scenario has them sitting there looking totally ridiculous in their underwear. DON'T BOTHER.

If you're going to make an inspired presentation you need to relate to your audience on a slightly more mature level. Think of it like this: you have important information to give out; your audience is presumably interested to hear what you have to say, or else they wouldn't be wasting their time attending. If you find visualisation techniques help, you'd be much better placed by cooking up a scenario that sees you giving a cracking performance to an audience of highly respected peers.

By the way, if you *are* still tempted by the old underpants trick, don't forget that when Homer Simpson tried it, he accidentally visualised himself looking down to reveal that he was *also* only wearing his underpants. Doh!

you
and your
client

It doesn't matter whether you call them clients or customers, if nobody buys your goods or services then you haven't got a business. It's as simple as that. Your clients need to be nurtured with care and respect. Your job is to educate them to a point where they wouldn't consider the idea of taking their business elsewhere.

THE COMPANY RULES

Rule 1   The customer is always right.

Rule 2   If the customer is wrong see Rule 1.

AS AN OFFICE CLICHÉ, that surely ranks with those little wooden plaques that announce "You don't have to be mad to work here… but it helps!" The fact is, though, every word of The Company Rules is true. Your clients are your bread and butter. Whatever the nature of your work, you forget that fact at your peril.

THE THREE P'S

The relationship you forge with your client should be of critical importance. If it isn't, then it probably won't last too long. Here are three words that should be able describe that relationship: PROFESSIONAL, PERSONAL and PRECISION. Have them tattooed on your brain if necessary.

PROFESSIONAL

The relationship between a self-employed person and his or her client could appear on the surface to be a rather one-sided one. Unless you are providing an absolutely unique service, your client will be able to choose from among you and any of your competitors. The client seems firmly in the driving seat. IT'S DOWN TO YOU TO CHANGE THIS PERCEPTION. Your ultimate fate as a business will depend on your ability to do this.

The most successful self-employed workers are those who prime themselves to exude professional quality at all times. So what is a "professional"? According to the Collins dictionary it's "a person who engages in an activity with great competence". Does that sounds like you in EVERY aspect of your work? This may seem a crass point, but the best way to win AND KEEP clients is by showing

> **❝** For my first consultancy job I worked in the IT department of a big insurance company. While I was there I got to know this rather brow-beaten young guy in his early 20s, who was working there as a part of "sandwich" course. He was given all the shitty jobs that nobody else would do, and generally treated like the scum of the earth. I sort of took him under my wing, helped him become more confident and soon realised that he had one very sharp brain. We kept in touch, and now, eight years on, he's a high flyer in the City. I'd estimate that in the past two years he's put at least £40,000 worth of business my way. It pays to be nice to people. **❞**
>
> **Michael Edwards, *management consultant***

**THE SECRETS OF
SELF-EMPLOYMENT
#27**
Giving feedback: "Too much criticism drains the mind. Keep the ratio of appreciation to criticism approximately five to one to keep the other person thinking well" – Nancy Kline, *Time to Think*.

through example that you are always in pursuit of that aim. Your goal should always to do the job in hand SO WELL that you leave your client both satisfied and deeply impressed. This strategy can NEVER fail. And it creates a knock-on effect: if you always make an impression on those with whom you come into contact, as they move on, they take your reputation along with them. That's more valuable than any CV can ever be.

Nothing breeds client confidence like a successful track record

There could be many specific reasons why you might win a contract over a competitor, but whatever they are, the bottom line is that the client must have CONFIDENCE in your ability to do the job, or provide the goods or services. Nothing breeds this confidence like the success of a good track record. If you do an excellent job once, you will be able to do it time and time again. So why would your client even bother looking at your competitors?

PERSONAL

Don't underestimate the importance of personal relationships in dealing with your clients. You could be the very essence of professionalism, but if your client doesn't "like" having you around then it won't bode too well for the future.

If you could dissect the personality traits of some of the world's most successful businessmen you'd notice that one thing they have in common is an ability to create an instant rapport with those around them. It's no great mystery that people with common interests like to mix socially. The same is true in the workplace. It's not exactly profound to suggest that we'd all prefer to spend work time with people that we like. It makes the day a little bit more enjoyable. It's clear, though, that some people have a natural edge. Confident, outgoing personalities tend to have more advanced interpersonal skills. ➡

Even if you are not naturally the life and soul of the office, you can still do a lot to alter negative communication traits. Here's a sensible list of dos and don'ts for when working at a client's office. Most of them seem to make obvious common sense, but too often the get ignored:

- **Always greet people. Make bodily contact (a handshake or pat on the back) if you think it's appropriate**
- **Always try to be friendly and polite**
- **Go out of your way to find common ground or interests – even if it's just discussing a football match by the water cooler.**
- **Avoid talking at length about yourself – make a point of asking (and remembering) details about those with whom you work**
- **Try to be seen as a problem solver rather than a problem bringer**

> ❝ Personal relationships are so vital for keeping alive business contacts. At the start of one job, during a casual conversation the manager that hired me confided that one of his childhood dreams was to own an E-type Jaguar – when my stint with this client had finished I sent him a little toy E-type. I'm told he keeps it in his office. That means that on his desk there's a constant reminder of my existence. ❞
> **Jon Etheridge, *freelance training officer***

- **Don't whinge about your work – that's the prerogative of the client's permanent staff**
- **Don't engage in company gossip**
- **Don't engage in company politics**
- **Don't engage in personal criticism – this will ALWAYS find its way back to you**
- **No self-employed person ever gained ANYTHING by being rude, unpleasant or aggressive to a client or a client's staff.**

PRECISION

Here's another veritable business cliché: MAKE SURE YOUR BRIEFS ARE AS TIGHT AS POSSIBLE. It's critical that you and your client understand in as much detail as possible what each can expect of the other. This is where your initial brief is so important. When you agree to undertake work, at the very least, it should be agreed:

- **EXACTLY what work has to be done**
- **EXACTLY when that work has to be completed (including interim dates)**
- **EXACTLY who has to approve or sign-off your work**
- **EXACTLY what (and when) you can expect to be paid for doing that work.**

Of course, in many instances, that information will be contained within a formal contract. If it isn't, though, ensure that you get it in writing in some shape or form. Informal arrangements may work satisfactorily in some industries, but at the end of the day, as Hollywood mogul Sam Goldwyn famous quoted, "A verbal contract's not worth the paper it's written on."

Armed with a schedule, the best thing you can now do for your reputation is hit those target dates. Even if the client doesn't ask for one, it's a good idea to provide a brief weekly progress report. It will enhance your client's confidence in your work. But if schedules look like being delayed, let the client know as soon as possible. ●

DO I NEED MORE THAN ONE CLIENT?

Every self-employed service provider starts off the same way, with a single client. It's not that uncommon for first-timers even to return to their previous permanent employer. But from that point, you should begin to create the seeds from which an effective network can bloom. Job turnover is vastly higher than it was even a decade ago, which means there are rich pickings out there for those with an eye for an opportunity.

One thing is certain, though, depending on a single source of income is a risky game, forcing you to flow with the fortunes of the company (or individual) who hired you. This does rather go against the grain of "self-determination" that appeals so strongly to so many of us. It can also be pretty boring always working for the same company. More dangerously, though, it can narrow your horizons. One of the reasons that self-employed staff are attractive to employers is precisely because they have varied experience.

So what is the ideal number of clients? There's no such thing – it clearly depends on the nature and volumes of the work you undertake for each one. However, juggling too many clients can be as risky as depending on just the one. And when workloads get too high you may find yourself having to say "no thanks" – something that grieves most self-employed workers. Consultant Jim Moore offers this advice: "One is too few… but a soloist doesn't need more than a few clients. I know some investment bankers who do only two deals a year." ●

Having too many clients can be as risky as having just one

CONTRACTORS BEWARE!

Many self-employed professionals spend a great deal of time working for a single client. Whilst this is normal when a business is getting off the ground, you need to be aware of a number of legal quirks that may take effect in the long run. The most infamous is the IR35 regulation, affecting one-man limited companies - for example, the "contractors" found in the IT and engineering industries.

In situations where you carry out your business on a client's premises, the government may deem you to be in "disguised employment". As a result, you can claim fewer legitimate business expenses, and will consequently pay significantly more in tax and National Insurance. Some critics would claim that this has contributed to an unprecedented recent brain drain of Britain's "Knowledge Workers".

The sad fact of IR35 is that it was brought into being as a way of *protecting* workers from unscrupulous employers who may make them redundant and then rehire them immediately as contract staff, thus avoiding statutory employee rights.

Some contractors have sought to circumvent IR35 by exchanging invoices among themselves for "training" or "consultancy". This is one way of broadening a client base! Unfortunately it's also illegal.

Although IR35 only affects limited companies, the Inland Revenue has similar "status" tests for sole traders.

This is complex area, and so if you have any doubts about how you may be affected it's a good idea to consult your accountant.

CLIENT MAINTENANCE

Even after you've won over a client, there is still plenty of maintenance work to be done if you are to get the best out of your working relationship. You shouldn't be providing services for one client the whole time, so it's important that during periods when you are out of your client's sight, you are not also out of his mind. This is where a combination of skilful organisation and a smart small-scale public relations strategy come into play.

YOUR CLIENT LOG

It's always a good idea to keep a record of your ongoing dealings with a client. All it takes is a simple two column page headed "Date" and "Action". Every time any event takes place – from a telephone conversation to an invoice payment – relating to one of your clients, you make a note of it. This provides you with a useful at-a-glance history of your relationship with the client. It can help you keep track of invoices (*see more about this on pages 112-113*), rates of pay, speed of payments, and much more besides.

A particularly useful function of your client log is that it can tell you when you and your were last in contact. This is a critical piece of information. Even if there is no desire or likelihood of you being engaged in the near future, you should never let more than three months pass without some form of communication.

KEEPING IN TOUCH

Maintaining periodic contact with a valuable client serves two functions. Firstly it acts as a reminder of your existence – this is of course critical. Secondly, however, by giving a rundown of your current activities and an indication of time you have free in the future, you're sending out an important message – that you're successful and your services are in demand.

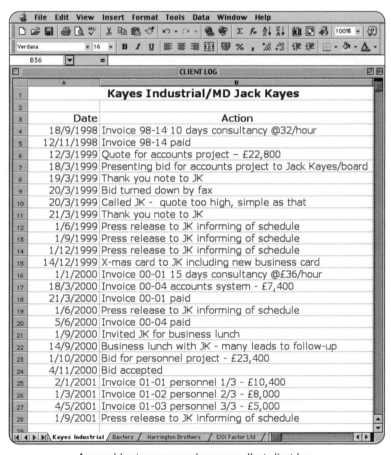

A spreadsheet program makes an excellent client log.

It doesn't require a long detailed letter, and, depending on your relationship with the client, it can be pretty informal. ●

Dear Jack,

I'm in the process of completing a project for Exx Factor Ltd. I just thought I'd let you know that over the next three months I currently have around 18 days free. Please let me know if I can be of service in any way.

Jeff Hargreaves

CLIENT INTELLIGENCE

A client needn't be the organisation. In some cases your client will, in effect, be an individual within a company. Or you may have several clients within the same office. This can make life a little more difficult: companies themselves remain relatively stable, whereas employees come and go. This makes it especially important to maintain a personal connection: a key member of staff changing jobs without your knowledge could be a disaster.

But if you know what's going on, you can use situations like this to your advantage. Try, for example, to get an introduction to your client's replacement (preferably from your client). And, above all, make sure that you know the details of your client's new company. If you play your cards right, instead losing a client you might actually keep the old one AND gain a new one. Persistent contact should keep you in the frame, but it also helps to maintain other social contacts within the company. For example, getting yourself invited to after-hours works drinking sessions can yield excellent results. Get Schmoozing! ●

THE SECRETS OF SELF-EMPLOYMENT #28

Winning a piece of work doesn't have to mean you'll get paid. Draw up and agree a proposal for payment before the work begins.

REWARDING YOUR CLIENTS?

In some areas of business there is a tradition for rewarding continued custom with a token of appreciation. But is this a good practice?

Remember, there is delicate dynamic to most kinds of relationship – yours with your client is no exception. If you go down this route, take care not to throw it off balance. Too big a gift might make the client feel embarrassed, uncomfortable, or if you're trying to buy favours; worst of all, it might make *you* look a bit desperate. On the other hand, too small a gift could be taken as an insult.

If you do give a gift, make sure that in your own mind it's a no-strings-attached deal. The best you should hope to get out of it is a closer personal relationship – and you may be able to achieve that just by sending a Christmas card.

For most purposes, the odd business lunch makes for a nice gesture, and has the advantage of allowing you to "talk shop" with your client. And in many cases, the favour will also be returned.

INVOICES AND PAYMENT

One issue guaranteed to get the veins bulging in even the most mild-mannered of self-employed workers is the thorny subject of payment. It's easy for permanent employees, they always know when payday is coming, but companies tend to treat their self-employed workforce in much the same way as any other supplier. That means they'll hang on to the money until the last possible moment, letting interest accrue nicely in their bank accounts. Here we'll look at some strategies to help get your hands on your money a little more swiftly.

INVOICES

Sometimes the Big Bad Company is not actually the culprit. Too many self-employed workers seem clueless as to the basic information that needs to go on an invoice. If you get this wrong, your invoice may not even be under consideration for payment. Here are the basics.

REMEMBER YOU'RE A PROFESSIONAL

Your invoice is a part of your personal "brand", so make sure that it looks the part. However "correct" the information on the page, tatty hand-written scraps of paper are more likely to end up in the rubbish bin than signed off for payment.

COMPANY PROTOCOL

Some accounts departments insist on a purchase order number having been allocated in advance. If this isn't shown on your invoice, you may not get paid. Other common non-statutory requirements may be Schedule D codes (*see page 53*) or details of your accountant. You have a much better chance

> **ff** One company I work for regularly takes three or four months to pay my invoices. They're a useful client, so I don't want to stir things up. My strategy is that whenever I quote a job for them I always add in a 5% overhead – I wouldn't necessarily charge that to other clients. It doesn't solve the problem, but at least I no longer feel I'm being ripped off! **JJ**
> **Karen Grant, *graphic designer***

of getting paid on time if accounts staff don't have to go to the trouble of finding extra information.

CONTENT

Your invoice should contain at least these details:

- **Company name and contact details**
- **Your name and contact details (if different)**
- **Invoice date**
- **Your own reference (the number that identifies this payment in your accounts)**
- **Client contact who commissioned the work**
- **Details of the work completed**
- **Invoice amount**
- **VAT amount, VAT rate and new total payable (if you are VAT registered)**
- **Your payment terms – the period within which you expect to be paid (yeah, right!)**

CHECK THE MATHS

Accounts staff usually check that the calculations you have made are correct. If they're not, your invoice is likely to find its way into a file marked "Pending" – this is the accounts department's equivalent to a black hole.

FINALLY, SEND IT TO THE RIGHT PERSON

Seems so obvious, doesn't it?

CHASING YOUR CHEQUES

Most of us really don't want to alienate our clients. Although this may sound like a cop-out, in practice we accept slow payment as a fact of life – especially when dealing with large businesses.

If we don't want to get tough, the next best thing is to get organised. The golden rule is to ALWAYS know who owes you money, and when it should be paid. When that cheque doesn't appear on time, that's when you make your first move.

GET ON THE PHONE

It's easy to get worked up about late payments, but shouting at the clerk responsible for processing your invoices won't do you much good. Surely it's more intelligent to try to forge a relationship with this person, isn't it? If you're on first-name terms, you'll get better information more quickly. By talking to the accounts department at this early stage you'll find out if your invoice has been lost. Make follow-up calls every fourteen days.

UNDERSTAND YOUR CLIENT

Find out as much as you can about your client's payment systems. Some have terribly convoluted methods for processing invoices. Each one may have to be signed off by any number of departments – that alone can double the time it takes for you to be paid. Furthermore, many large companies have just one monthly cheque run. If you miss that, you have no chance of being paid until the next one.

MONTHLY STATEMENTS

If you have a number of invoices floating through your client's system, it may be worth your while sending out monthly statements detailing invoice numbers, amounts and due dates.

BRINGING IN THE LAW

You should only resort to legal action when you've tried everything else. Think carefully before you go down this route. After all, it's certain to end your working relationship with that client. Does that bother you? If you operate in a close-knit industry, you may also suddenly find yourself with a reputation for being "difficult" – however unfair that may be. Weigh up the odds before you make such a move.

Your next destination is the small claims court. You don't need to get a solicitor involved, but simply complete a form, pay a fee (which depends on the amount being claimed) and lodge it with your client's local debtor's court.

INTEREST

Under the 1998 Late Payments of Commercial Debts (Interest) Act, you are legally entitled to charge interest at the base rate plus eight percent on any overdue payments. This action holds the same caveats as the box above.

THE SECRETS OF SELF-EMPLOYMENT #29

Say no, but pause with sincerity first – it gives you a chance to think and your client the benefit of consideration.

keeping
it
together

5

in this chapter...

time to kill?

Getting organised means making the most effective use of your time. That doesn't mean working harder, but — as the cliche goes — working *smarter*. There's more to time management, however, than just learning how to use a diary. It strikes at the very soul of the way you go about your work.

FOR SOME PEOPLE, the idea of time management is anathema. They carry out their daily tasks with a macrocosmic view that focuses only on a distant end date. The way their time is structured within that schedule may be quite arbitrary. Of course, most of us know from experience what happens next — as students, how many of us started a lengthy assignment only a couple of days before it was due to be handed in?

A solid understanding (and practice) of time management is useful for so many reasons:

- You can plan your days and weeks in detail
- It helps you to turn long-term goals into achievable daily targets
- It removes a layer of uncertainty and stress from your working life
- You can make more efficient use of your time and energy in and out of work
- It gives you a greater degree of personal control
- It allows you to identify persistent time-wasting elements in your day
- It eventually becomes easier to make more realistic timing estimates. ●

> 66 I've been on several time management courses, but I've never really managed to get very much out of them. The problem was they all seemed geared towards getting me to fill out every last 15-minute period in my calendar — even scheduling in leisure time. It's just so restricting. I just don't work that way. Sure, some things have to be done at certain times, but I think there's a lot of value in leaving space for something spontaneous to happen. 99
> **Martina Chong,** *designer*

	URGENT	NOT URGENT
IMPORTANT	**1** ● Crises ● Problems requiring immediate attention ● Deadline-driven events	**2** ● Planning and development ● Forming relationships ● Goal formation ● Recreation
NOT IMPORTANT	**3** ● Interruptions ● Mail, telephone, etc ● Most meetings ● Routine reports	**4** ● Trivial activities ● Time-wasting activities ● Some mail ● Some telephone calls

UNDERSTANDING OUR TASKS

What is that governs what the things we do at any given time? Although there can any number of specific reasons, it ultimately boils down to two factors: URGENCY and IMPORTANCE.

Urgent tasks are those that shout out for our attention. They may be genuine all-hands-on-deck emergencies, tasks with short deadlines attached, someone banging on the door, or the telephone ringing. They may not have the same strategic value but they all require something to be done immediately. The important tasks are those to which we attribute high personal priorities (or have such priorities placed on them on our behalf). These are the jobs whose outcomes have greater *meaning*.

All tasks – everything that we ever do – can be ascribed both a degree of urgency and importance. The diagram above is what author Stephen Cavey calls the "Time Management Matrix". The rows represent tasks that can be categorised as being either important or not important; the columns show tasks that are either urgent or not urgent. Each of the four quadrants represents different combinations of these two factors.

> **All tasks – everything that we ever do – can be ascribed a degree of urgency and importance**

THE URGENT LIST

Let's start by looking at Quadrant 1. This describes tasks that are both urgent and important. These are the high-priority tasks that require our immediate attention. This is fire-fighting mode. If we spend most of our time on Quadrant 1 tasks we resign ourselves to a life of stress, exhaustion and burnout. This is where life's crisis managers can be found. These are the people who confuse hard work with being effective. Some of these people can even have skewed ideas as to what actually constitutes important: they may think that they're dealing with Quadrant 1 tasks, but are actually devoting their energy to Quadrant 3 – urgent tasks that have little importance.

THE UNIMPORTANT LIST

There are, of course, many who spend most of their time in Quadrants 3 and 4 dealing with non-important issues. These are the least effective people of all. They can only focus on the short term, and have little real conception of the idea of prioritisation, planning time and forming long-term goals.

THE EFFECTIVE LIST

The most personally effective people (and the ones that consequently lead the most satisfying lives) are those that focus on what is important rather than what is necessarily urgent. These Quadrant 2 tasks are the most important of all. They deal with issues such as our future vision – planning and development – taking preventative

> **WHERE DOES *YOUR* DAY GO?**
>
> How good a time manager do you think you are? Before we move on look at ways in which you can improve your effective time management, let's take a look at your current working practices. Across the page you'll see a time log. It's a standard working day divided into 15-minute segments. Make five photocopies of this page. Every day for the next working week, you must fill in a copy. Enter ABSOLUTELY EVERYTHING you do, from working through the heftiest report to taking a coffee break. We'll take a look at the results on page 120.

action, forging relationships, building our goals and valuable recreation. This is where most of our action should be taking place.

If there is an art of time management it's the way in which we balance the four quadrants. The main difficulty most of us have is finding time for the important Quadrant 2 tasks. This is because we are called upon to REACT to the urgent tasks. Whether or not they are important, these tasks *happen* and we *respond*. Quadrant 2 tasks, however, require us to be PROACTIVE – we have to make these things happen for ourselves. This requires discipline. Nobody, of course, is suggesting that we shouldn't deal with urgent important tasks. That would be absurd. The inference is merely that if we spend our time constantly reacting to what goes on around us, we never make time to do the things that *we* want to do.

The most effective people are those that focus on what is important rather than what is necessarily urgent

YOUR TIME TEST

DATE:

8:00		**14:00**	
8:15		14:15	
8:30		14:30	
8:45		14:45	
9:00		**15:00**	
9:15		15:15	
9:30		15:30	
9:45		15:45	
10:00		**16:00**	
10:15		16:15	
10:30		16:30	
10:45		16:45	
11:00		**17:00**	
11:15		17:15	
11:30		17:30	
11:45		17:45	
12:00		**18:00**	
12:15		18:15	
12:30		18:30	
12:45		18:45	
13:00		**19:00**	
13:15		19:15	
13:30		19:30	
13:45		19:45	

ANALYSING YOUR TIME

When you've completed about a week's worth of time tests you can begin to analyse how well you are spending your work time. What we are going to do is calculate how much of your day is taken up with each of these three main work categories: ROUTINE TASKS, such as making telephone calls, attending regular meetings, writing regular reports or dealing with e-mails; ONGOING PROJECTS; and PLANNING AND DEVELOPMENT. Before you begin, make an estimate based on gut feel of what you think the likely proportions are going to be. Write down those figures.

Now take three different coloured highlighter pens, one representing each of the three categories. Look at each 15-minute minute segment for each day, and select the category most relevant to the activity you've written down. Highlight it with

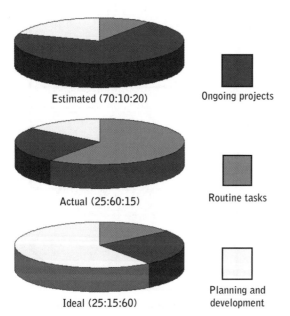

Estimated (70:10:20)

Ongoing projects

Actual (25:60:15)

Routine tasks

Ideal (25:15:60)

Planning and development

WASTED TIME = WASTED CASH

One way or another, most self-employed people cost out their time on an hourly rate. It follows, then, that if you are wasting time you are also wasting money (or at least potential earnings).

Here's a scary exercise for you to try out. Take one of your time logs and count up the number of "wasted" minutes throughout the day. Now perform this calculation:

$$\frac{\text{HOURLY RATE}}{60} \times \text{WASTED MINUTES}$$

This is how much your wastage cost on that day. If it's a typical day, you can multiply that figure by 20 to see your wastage for a month.

the appropriately coloured pen. The three categories should account for all of your time with the exception of lunch breaks. Once you have worked through all of your time logs, make a total of the time spent engaged in each category for the entire week. Express each one as a percentage of the total available time. Compare the results to your estimate.

Research suggests that most of us have a pretty poor perception of how we *really* use our time. We may think of ourselves devoting most energy to dealing with ongoing projects (*see top left*). The reality is usually somewhat different: more than half of the time, most of us are engaged in routine tasks (*see centre left*) – the category that incorporates most of our wastage.

The most successful time managers spend the greater part of their day on development (*see bottom left*) – classic Quadrant 2 tasks. They rightly believe that no time spent on planning is ever wasted.

TIME STEALERS

Studying your time logs is the best way to identify recurrent areas that may eat into your time without your realisation. Here are some of the biggest offenders.

MEETINGS

Most meetings are a waste of time. For the self-employed that can also mean a loss of income – you rarely get paid for meetings that relate to future possible work. To keep things as efficient as possible it's always a good idea to tell the participants at the start of the meeting how much time you have available – this gives you a get-out clause if things begin to drag.

THE INTERNET

Minutes can turn into hours when playing around with e-mail and surfing the World Wide Web. Try to keep all your electronic communications as short as possible. If you don't have a permanently connected line, get into the habit of logging on to the Internet at specific times – for example, ONLY checking for mail every hour on the hour.

SURPRISE VISITORS

Personal relationships are especially important to the self-employed, from both social and business perspectives, Indeed, we should make time to encourage their development. Sometimes, however, unwarranted interruptions can become major time stealers. It requires considerable tact and diplomacy to "throw someone out" without being offensive. Some ensure that there is no permanent provision for additional seating in their office – if unwanted visitors can't make themselves comfortable they're less likely to stay!

It's a different matter when you work from home. You may find that friends and family take your work time less seriously than when you had a permanent job. Although it's imperative to make time for those close to us, we also need to educate them the way we choose to work. And that can be tough. (Although you don't have to end up like Jack Nicholson in *The Shining*: "Whenever you hear me typing, STAY THE F*** OUT!")

The more you separate your business life from your home life – even while still working at home – the less of a problem this is likely to be.

THE TELEPHONE

This may be the biggest offender of them all. Although it's a critically important business tool, it's equally important to our social lives, and the two uses can easily become intermingled. Of course, nobody is suggesting that you don't take or make social calls during your working hours – you didn't quit permanent employment to subject yourself to such rigid rules – but you should beware of the amount of time it can eat up:

- **Try to keep business calls from turning into social calls**
- **When you make the call you set the agenda. Once you've achieved your aims, politely end the call**
- **If you take a personal call during a busy period, give a preset limit for the time you have free: "I'm a bit tied up, but I can talk for a couple minutes."**
- **When you're *very* busy, take the phone off the hook, or switch it to voicemail mode.** ●

JUST CAN'T SAY "NO"?

We self-employed types are a funny lot, aren't we? We just love to say "Yes". We all want to make our clients or colleagues happy, don't we? And how often does it get us into deep water? Too often. There are plenty reasons why we do this: some are closely connected with the relationships we have with our clients, but others are more a matter of personality.

> **Some people are so poorly organised that they don't actually know how much free time they can spare**

I'LL NEVER WORK AGAIN!

The simple act of being unable to turn work away is the main reason that so many self-employed people can't bring themselves to utter those two magic letters. It's an understandable (if not always logical) state of mind that we could call the "I'll-never-work-again syndrome". And you'll be surprised at how many successful, experienced independent workers – some earning huge incomes – live with the fear that when the current contract is over, work will dry up. Some people just can't help but think that way. If that's you, it's no use pretending there's an easy way around it – the best consolation is that the more experience you gain the less likely it is to be such an issue.

MR AND MRS HELPFUL

Some people are always ready to lend a hand – even if it means delaying more important work of their own. If that describes you, then you are clearly a very nice person. Very nice indeed. The trouble with being perceived this way in your work is that others can take advantage of you. They may just assume that you will sort things out for them. Learn to put your own work first. If you genuinely have the time then by all means get stuck in, otherwise it's: "I'm sorry, I can't leave what I'm doing just now, but if it can wait until tomorrow morning I'll gladly take a look."

MR AND MRS KNOW-ALL

Of course, some people just don't *want* to say "no". They are the office experts. They *need* to feel important. They *need* to feel needed. If that's you, try to stay focussed on the work you're supposed to be doing. If you have to show off in an office environment, make sure it's by being good at that.

ARE YOU FREE?

A system that gained some currency during the 1980s was the notion of "green" and "red" time. The principle is based around the idea that when planning your time you allocate certain sections of each day in which under no circumstances you can be disturbed. These are your work-intense periods. In offices, staff using this system may refer to it as "red" time (some even put up little red signs on their office doors); the rest of the time is "green".

Although that might all sound a bit silly, there is good sense in booking yourself quiet time. It allows you to build a dynamic to your working day – call it your "power" time, if you will. Put the telephone into voicemail mode, switch off your e-mail and get your head down (to work, that is – not sleep).

I CAN PROBABLY FIT IT IN

Some can't turn down work because they are so poorly organised that they don't actually know how much free time they can spare. This is shamefully common. And unnecessary. If your time is well planned on a daily, weekly and monthly basis, this needn't be an issue. When someone offers you work, you take a look at your commitments. If you're at capacity, it's: "sorry, I really can't take any more work on just now."

That, however, may be easier said than done, because…

I DON'T WANT TO UPSET MY CLIENT

When you're self-employed it can be easy to take on the belief that the client is all-powerful, and that you are somehow privileged to have been chosen to perform tasks on his or her behalf. Consequently, you bend over backwards to accommodate unreasonable requests.

This is a dangerous practice. As well as playing havoc with your planned time, it sets a poor precedent. And routinely dealing with unreasonable demands as a way of impressing a client may backfire as a strategy – you may just up the level of expectation. Whoever you are, whatever do, never forget that **you have the right to refuse a client's excessive demands on your time**. Try, if you can, to turn these demands back on your client. For example, "I can do that, but it will delay the work I'm currently doing for you." But even more impressive to most clients would be "… but I know someone else who might be able to help with this problem. Would you like me to give her a call?" ●

WEB CONTACTS

Time management is big business. You can tell from the number of professional websites devoted to the subject. Here is a small selection. In most cases the name of the website is evident from the URL:

www.tmi.co.uk
   Time Manager International
www.gettingagripontime.com
www.mindtools.com
www.balancetime.com
www.bigtimes.co.uk
www.businesstown.com
www.smartbiz.com
www.timedoctor.com
www.stress.about.com/cs/timemanagement
www.isbister.com
   Time & Choas software
www.journals.about.com/timemanagement
www.timemaster.net

THE SECRETS OF SELF-EMPLOYMENT #30

If you can't help but abuse your email system, packages such as Retriever help you index, sort and find your email.

getting organised

It was said that Albert Einstein never even tried to remember dull stuff like addresses or appointments. As long it was written down somewhere then why waste effort storing it away in the mind? The important thing was that, unlike many of us, he had a *system* in place to cover the efficient processing and flow of information.

MANY PEOPLE GO about their daily tasks in what seems to be a more-or-less random fashion. They scratch their heads, the brain ticks for a moment, and then a new task is plucked out of the air. This is not to say that they're no good what they do, or even that they are ineffective. Merely that by relying mostly on memory they are not operating in the smartest way.

To be well organised you need a system for dealing with the flow of information

To be organised you need a system is place for dealing with the the flow of information. Think of it as an assembly line. Every time a piece of paper reaches your desk, it ought to be "sent" somewhere else for storage or processing. You can always tell those who don't have a system: they're the ones whose desks have almost no visible surface space – it's mostly a mysterious mound of paperwork. It doesn't mean that no work gets done, it's just that even the simplest of tasks become that little bit more difficult and stressful – and don't ask them to find a specific document from those piles or you'll be waiting all day.

If this sounds painfully familiar to you, there are some steps you can follow that will hopefully transform your environment into something a little more work-friendly.

> **❝** The best thing I ever bought was a whiteboard. It's fixed to the wall in front of my desk. First job in the morning is scrawling the key tasks of the day on the board in HUGE letters. It's a constant reminder. **❞**
> **Marco Baceo,** *importer*

A NEW BROOM

It helps to sort your work as it comes in. The following method is just one way of organising your space. But it's as good a starting point as any other. As you go about your work, you'll be able to personalise the system.

By ordering your in-tray into the following distinct categories, it will help you to prioritise your work.

● **Immediate action** For documents that have to be dealt with by the end of the day

● **Non-urgent** Documents that must be dealt with by the end of the week

● **File** Documents that have been dealt with and are ready to be moved to a filing system

● **Reading** Information of possible interest but requiring no direct action.

Anything that doesn't fit your in-tray goes straight in the bin. After you've done this for the first time, your desk will be both clean and tidy. But creating order is not a one-off 'spring-cleaning' task. It requires a change in your working habits. It's a smart idea to set aside a specific time each day to deal with your in-tray. Naturally, the immediate action in-tray always takes priority, but you should also make a point of checking the non-urgent items on a daily basis – at some point they are going to become urgent. The one you need to watch, though, is the file tray. If left, this will quickly get out of control.

Filing is the most tedious job in the world.

> ❝ One of the tips I picked on my time-management course was the "two-bin trick". You have two wastepaper bins, one marked "RUBBISH" and one marked "POSSIBLE RUBBISH". Anything you know to be rubbish goes in the first bin; anything you're not quite sure about goes in the second bin. The theory is that if you have a well-thought-out system for filing documents, and those "possibles" don't fit into it, then they have no use anyway. At the end of the day you empty the second bin into the first, and throw the lot away! ❞
> **Dr Raj Patel, *physicist***

but it has to be done. Try to get into the habit of dealing with your in-tray during those low-key moments between key tasks, or when you have the odd 15 minutes to spare.

The rules for applying a system to your in-tray also apply to the 'virtual' desk on your computer. Get into the habit of storing documents in logically named folders rather than leaving them to run loose on your desktop. ●

THE SECRETS OF SELF-EMPLOYMENT #31
The 80-20 rule: Practise imperfection – understand when you can achieve the results required with the minimum of effort.

YOUR TASK LIST

How do you judge the success of a working day? Many of us seem to equate productivity with how busy we've been. But how good a measure of achievement is that *really*? After all, a hamster on a treadwheel exerts a whole lot of energy, but never actually gets very far. And that just about sums up a day at work for many of us.

> **Every working day should start in exactly the same way – either studying or compiling a task list**

SETTING GOALS

Time for another business cliche: **if you don't know where you're going, how will you know when you've arrived?** What all of us require on a daily basis is a set of achievable goals. This will help bring structure and meaning to our activities. This is precisely what your task list is all about.

Every working day should start in exactly the same way. You either study or compile a task list. Working as an adjunct to your desk diary, this document provides you with your short-term goals – the things that have to be done today. Your task list can be written on a piece of paper, a computer file or on a huge whiteboard next to your desk. It doesn't matter what it looks like as long as it's there.

LIST MAINTENANCE

You should refer to your task list constantly during the course of the day, making amendments, altering priorities or ticking off items as they are completed. Indeed, for some people, this act in itself can be a major motivator – it provides them with at-a-glance proof that the day is going according to their plan.

To be truly effective, every task on your list should be:

- **Measurable**
- **Achievable**
- **Prioritisable**

You should be able to estimate how long each will take, and when you intend to do the work; the list should be realistic about what it's possible to do in a single day; it should be obvious which are the most important items on the list.

> ❝ As an industrial relations specialist, I'm often called in when a board has lost faith in one of its departments. But whatever the specific problems, there always a seems to be a common element – I'd describe it as a culture that promotes reaction rather than proaction. It usually stems from a management sceptical of the value of directing resources into the planning function. These people fail to understand that planning should be a daily issue for everybody... the end result is always the same – confusion. No matter who they are – senior or junior, experienced or novice – when people don't know *exactly* what they are trying to achieve on a daily basis, they'll eventually drift into unfocussed activity. ❞
>
> **Mark Hofner,** *management consultant*

PRIORITISATION

Every task you set yourself must also come with some indication of its importance or urgency. Every item on your task list can be placed into one of three categories:

● **A-TASKS** These are tasks that are both important AND urgent;

● **B-TASKS** These are tasks that are either important OR urgent, but not both;

● **C-TASKS** These are your routine tasks – they are NEITHER important nor urgent.

When planning your working day, always try to go for a good mixture of A-, B- and C-tasks. Try to avoid creating days that are made up entirely from one type: a whole day of A-tasks will be so intense that your concentration is sure to waver; a day of low-level C-tasks may well leave you feeling bored and unfulfilled.

Energy levels can differ widely from person to person. So when scheduling your list, consider the times of the day when you usually experience energy peaks, and reserve them for A-tasks.

ACCURACY

Each time you complete a piece of work, get into the habit of comparing your estimate to the amount of time it actually took to perform the task. The more information you can compile about your ability as a time manager, the better equipped you will be to bring about changes in your performance. ●

REALITY CHECK

If a cartoonist ever wanted to create a a super-hero aimed at the self-employed it would have to be THE AMAZING TIME-EXPANDING MAN. There's no question that some of us have a pretty distorted view of how much we can pack into a single day. Frankly, none of us benefits from failing to achieve an unrealistic set of daily goals – we just end up exhausted and demoralised. And we're not much fun to be around when that happens.

With a realistic awareness of our capabilities we can take on daily tasks with confidence – and when we need to stretch ourselves we know we can do so without going into stress overload. Comparing actual performance with estimates is one foolproof way of assessing how close we are to our limits.

Don't forget that priorities may change during the course of a day

---

THE SECRETS OF SELF-EMPLOYMENT #32

If you're part of a virtual project team, use services such as www.projectplace.co.uk to successfully manage the project

PROJECT PLANNING

"One man can eat the largest water buffalo — one mouthful at a time."

Arapaho Indian expression

The art of time management and project planning go hand in hand. The basic principles of planning revolve around the idea of breaking down a large task into a series of smaller tasks. Indeed, this is the only way we can accurately predict how long it will take for a major task to be completed.

By dividing a lengthy and weighty task into smaller units we not only learn in detail exactly WHAT has to be done, and in what sequence, but we are also in a better position to accurately estimate its COST in terms of time and/or money.

By creating a critical path – the greatest number of dependent steps between the start and finish – and totalling the elapsed time each task

The theory behind project planning is based on logic and breaking tasks down into manageable sizes.

If it's an area that you feel you're weak in and will need to be strong in, it could be worth looking at a course in project management.

There are also many software packages designed to help you manage projects.

If you're likely to be working with a client who uses these, it's worth getting yourself acquainted with them.

will take, we can produce a much more accurate estimate of the time it will take for the project (the major task) to be completed.

The benefit of planning by breaking down large tasks into smaller components becomes more evident the larger the project and available labour resources.

By dividing a task into smaller units we can estimate more accurately how long it will take to complete

This will highlight which tasks are dependent on others before they can begin. For instance, a decorator wouldn't begin to paint a wall before the plaster had set. Once you've identified these dependencies, you can create a realistic timetable for your project.

It's as well to cut some slack when estimating how long each task will take, to allow you some contingency. Although people will always want work done as quickly as possible, it is worse to let a client down on agreed timings.

> ❝ I have an undergraduate degree from Harvard and a graduate school degree from Princeton. But the most practically useful course I've ever taken was a week-long series of seminars on time planning. Some of my colleagues thought it amusing that I could spend a week 'learning how to use a diary', but I'm operating much more efficiently as a result. ❞
>
> **Mike Storner, *investment banker***

20 TOP ORGANISATIONAL TIPS

1. Do one thing at a time. Keep an overview of subsequent work on your task list.

2. When you start a piece of work, try to complete it at one sitting. Every time you pick up an unfinished task you have to "warm-up" again – this is a waste of your time.

3. Learn to say "no".

4. Periodically analyse your time. Look for patterns of wastage or inefficient practice.

5. We all have different metabolisms. Some of us are more effective at certain times of the day. Schedule the most demanding tasks to times of the day when you are likely to be at your best.

6. Try to create daily routine for dealing with routine tasks.

7. Avoid habitually taking your work home or, if you work at home, outside of your work zone. When work starts to impinge on your leisure time, frustration usually results.

8. Prioritise the items on your task list. Put off anything that isn't important.

9. Write down ideas the moment they come to you. Store them in a central source.

10. Never keep important information exclusively on "yellow stickies". It will get lost.

11. Avoid putting off unpleasant but important tasks. They will play on your mind.

12. Always plan before you act. Then put your plans into immediate action.

13. Breaking down major tasks into smaller components improves your overall understanding, and makes it easier to estimate and manage.

14. To avoid the unpleasant effects of stress, ensure that your daily goals are achievable.

15. Know when to let go of a finished task – avoid wasting time by tinkering.

16. Make sure that every task you have written down has a deadline.

17. Set out specific times when you don't want to be disturbed. Tell your colleagues.

18. Watch out for the time stealers such as the e-mail, the Web and telephone calls.

19. Keep your workspace tidy at all times.

20. Don't let your in-tray overflow.

stress

When the human body has to work beyond it's normal capabilities, the result is stress. Here are some tips on recognising the symptoms and keeping it under control.

WITHOUT STRESS, few of us would bother trying to achieve anything out of the ordinary – we wouldn't study hard for our exams, burn the candle at both ends to finish off an important job, or train every day for months for that marathon run. Problems start when it gets out of control. "Stress puppies" can end up with numerous physical and mental illnesses. Stress can even be a killer: the Japanese recognise this condition as *karoshi* – a term that describes death from work-related stress.

After decades of being swept under the carpet as a "wuss" condition, the importance of stress control is finally being acknowledged, especially since it's thought that at least 60% of absenteeism in the UK is a result of a stress-related disorder.

STRESS: WHAT IT DOES TO YOU

When your body is placed under either physical or psychological stress, it responds by increasing the production of hormones such as adrenaline and cortisol. This causes a change in heart rate, blood pressure and metabolism. In the short term this makes your body perform more efficiently – it's the prolonged boosting of these hormones that causes eventual damage.

RECOGNISING THE SYMPTOMS

There is no one single symptom that can identify stress. Some, such as heart disease and high blood pressure, can be life threatening.

Here is a list of some of the most common stress-related symptoms. If you are seriously suffering, there's a strong likelihood that you'll be experiencing more than one of these conditions:

- Insomnia
- Fatigue
- Headaches
- Skin disorders
- Digestive disorders
- Dramatic alteration in eating habits
- Becoming over-emotional in highly charged situations
- Gradual decline in personal appearance and hygiene
- Poor concentration
- Loss of confidence
- Increased consumption of alcohol, tobacco, caffeine or other drugs
- Breathlessness
- Drying in the mouth
- Dramatic mood swings

STRATEGY 1: WORK

As a breed, if we self-employed have one fault, it's a natural tendency to take on too much work (or at least agree to do too much, too quickly): we want to make our clients happy, but that can sometimes be to our own detriment. Taking on board some of the organisational techniques shown earlier in the chapter should help you to prevent stress getting out of control.

Knowing when to say "no" is a valuable skill to develop. That will help you to keep your work loads manageable. Also, the more planning you can do upfront the more certainty you will create in your working day. Uncertainty (often brought about by change) is one of the most significant causes of stress. Sufferers frequently report a sense of their lives drifting out of control. If you can sit down at your desk at the start of the day and say to yourself "I know *exactly* what I have to do", and use time management techniques to ensure they get done, half the battle is won.

Of course, The Big One is simply all about business survival. There's no simple answer here. Peaks and troughs are the very essence of the world we have chosen to inhabit. It makes no difference if they've been working that way for twelve months or twelve years, any self-employed person who claims NEVER to worry about where the next job is coming from is either extraordinarily thick-skinned (highly unlikely) or being economical with the truth (very likely). The harsh reality is that if the insecurity of this lifestyle actually damages your health, then you probably shouldn't be doing it. ➞

THE SECRETS OF SELF-EMPLOYMENT #33
"Stress is not the event, it's our perception of it" – Dr Hans Selye. Frame situations differently by thinking rationally.

Uncertainty is one of most significant stress creators

·DON'T WORRY – BE HAPPY

There seems to be plenty of evidence that those with a happy home life and a fulfilling social life are less likely to be affected by stress. Where core values have been prioritised, the conflicting demands on time are put into perspective. In short, surrounding yourself in low-stress environment away from work is one of the best ways of preventing stress getting out of control in the first place. So have fun – that's an order!

The big problem with work-related stress is that it rarely confines itself to the workplace. When we let it spill out into our family lives that can spell BIG TROUBLE. *Your* stress can easily be transmitted to a husband, wife, partner or children. If your other half also has a demanding career the difficulties may be multiplied. The high divorce rates we experience in the West are in part a result of stress.

Finally, if you *are* seriously overworked, and getting stressed out over deadlines, try going back to the client. Be straight. Say you need more time. We know that most clients want their work completed yesterday (or sooner), but even if they can't accommodate your request, it singles you out as being honest, and caring about your work. If that doesn't wash, the only real solution is to hire in some extra help (*see pages 134-137*).

But the bottom line is this: when work and health come head to head there ought only ever be one winner. ●

STRATEGY 2: MIND AND BODY

Keeping stress at bay requires holistic thinking. Treating your body right will also help to keep you in peak mental condition. Here are some strategies that can help.

EXERCISE

Stress can takes its physical toll. You can combat this with regular exercise. A work out at the gym, an aerobics class or a session in the swimming pool before, during or after your work will help you to fight fatigue and reduce tension. Even if you can't get to a gym, try to take periodic breaks from sitting at your desk. Some useful office exercises are shown across the page.

RELAXATION

Some of us find it hard to relax at the best of times. Here are some techniques – ancient and modern – that are worth considering:

WEB CONTACTS

www.floatworks.com
　　　　　UK's main floatation centre
www.counselling.co.uk
　　　　　Register of counsellors
www.bsh1950.co.uk
　　　　　British Society of Hypnotherapists
www.isma.co.uk
　　　　　Int. Stress Management Association
www.bwg.org.uk
　　　　　British Wheel of Yoga
www.int-fed-aromatherapy.co.uk
　　　　　Int. Fed. of Aromatherapists

● **Yoga** An ancient Indian self-help system that will improve both mental and physical help. Although there are many books available, it's a good idea to start with qualified instructor.

● **Alexander Technique** This popular system was devised by an Australian actor to help improve body posture.

● **Floatation** If laying in pool of warm salty water in total silence and total darkness sounds weird to you, think again. Even if you're not stressed out, give it a go – you won't regret it. Strongly recommended.

● **Reflexology** At the end of a hard day, what could be nicer than having your partner massaging your soles, stimulating the blood supply, muscles and relieving tension. There are plenty of DIY books and videos available.

Treating your body right will help to keep you in peak mental condition

- **Aromatherapy** Essential oils are extracted from plants or spices and either inhaled or gently massaged. For the best results use a qualified practitioner.

- **Hypnotherapy** Through suggestion, the hypnotherapist "guides" a patient into a relaxed state. Instructions are posted into the unconscious mind which aim to take effect when the patient regains consciousness. Some also find self-hypnosis relaxation tapes useful.

- **Counselling** There are many different types of counselling, but essentially it means talking through your problems with a professional listener. Just being able to discuss your problems with family and friends can often help you to put things into perspective.

- **Shiatsu** This is a massage treatment which works on the muscles, skin and soft tissue to release energy and relieve tension. •

THE SECRETS OF SELF-EMPLOYMENT #34

"I worked out the worst thing that could happen, which was that I'd run out of money and I'd have to go back and live with my mum"
Simon Woodroffe — *The Book of Yo!*

EXERCISE WHILE YOU WORK

Your body responds physically to stress. Minimising tension while you work can help to reduce the harmful effects of stress. Here is a series of exercises that can be performed without you even having to leave your office chair.

Exercise 1
Place your left hand on your right shoulder, and squeeze slowly and gently. Hold for a few seconds, then release. Now repeat for the opposite side.

Exercise 2
Bring the fingers of both hands behind your head to the base of your skull. Make slow, gentle circular movements, working gradually down your neck and across the shoulders.

Exercise 3
Place both hands flat on your shoulders. Breathe out and let your head fall backwards. Slowly bring your fingers over your collar bones.

Exercise 4
Place one hand on your chest and the other on your stomach. Breathe in slowly through the nose. Hold your breath for about 10 seconds. Exhale quickly through your mouth.

Exercise 5
Lift your left shoulder and slowly rotate it backwards. Repeat with the right shoulder, and then both shoulders together.

Exercise 6
Place your hands on the top of your head. Let your hands pull your head down gently until you feel a slight pinch at the back of your neck.

making
decisions

Whether it's choosing which socks to put on in the morning, determining the fate of an accused murderer in court, or trying to justify buying that cool convertible Merc, the very fabric of our lives is entwined within the decisions we continually make.

BUT LET'S NOT over-philosophise. In the context of business, the ability to make measured, rational judgements – sometimes on the spur of the moment – can be a critical factor in your ultimate success or failure. Like public orators, there are some who seem blessed with an unnatural ability for making split-second judgements – George W. Bush is reputed never to spend more than ten minutes making a decision. That might not be so tough when you're surrounded by teams of very smart advisors who've done most of the work for you, but when you're self-employed there are special implications – you have to make all those decisions by yourself. Do you accept a contract? Do you hire an accountant? Do you work from home or hire an office? If you make the wrong choice it can cost you time, money and clients.

The ability to make measured, rational judgements may be a crucial factor in your ultimate success or failure

REMOVE THE FEAR

How do you feel when you have a major decision to face? If you're like most of us, at the very least there will be anxiety – possibly outright fear. This is not so surprising given that we have a cultural view that mistakes and failures reflect badly on ourselves, rather than treating them as a fundamental part of the learning process.

But fear is bad for decision making. It affects the way we think (it actually takes up more brain space) which can lead us to take familiar or soft options. It can also made us "impression manage": we do this when we make decisions based around what others will think of us.

The most successful decision-makers are the ones who manage to remove the fear from the

SWOT ANALYSIS

SWOT is a marketing term. It is an acronym for STRENGTHS, WEAKNESSES, OPPORTUNITIES and THREATS. It is a very simple tool for analysing the essential business qualities of either a person, product or organisation.

Engaging in your own personalised SWOT study can improve your decision-making skills, and help to identify future career directions or training needs.

S What are you good at? Should you direct your working life accordingly?

W What are you not good at? Should you ignore it or rectify through training?

O Have you identified new business opportunities?

T Are aspects of your working life under threat from competitors, poor working practices or market and/or economic conditions?

process. There are a number of courses of action that can be taken to reduce the anxiety element.

PLAN AHEAD

You can circumvent a certain amount of anxiety by thinking in advance what you would do in a certain situation. These can be big, important decisions such as negotiating prices, or such small matters as deciding on the circumstances that you won't answer your mobile phone. The more everyday eventualities you can cover in this way the fewer decisions you'll have to work through on a daily basis.

ACCENTUATE THE POSITIVE

Going back to Susan Jeffers' "No-Lose" model (*see page 37*), instead of weighing up all of the pros and cons, or resorting to "what-ifs" like so many of us do – and for situations where there are different measurable outcomes this is a reasonable approach – we could choose to concentrate on the positive outcomes of each option. In this way, all decisions can have a satisfactory outcome. This approach is probably best left to philosophical changes rather than dealing with financial issues.

THE SECRETS OF SELF-EMPLOYMENT #35

Most decision conflicts are caused by lack of confidence and fear of a disastrous outcome. The combination of the intuition of experience and logical analysis will provide you with a sound basis on which to make your decisions.

POOR DECISIONS

It can be dangerous when decisions are overtaken by our natural enthusiasm. There is a need to see the practical consequences of an outcome if we are to avoid blind optimism. If you feel yourself falling into this trap, bounce your thoughts off colleagues – not the "yes men", but those you know will give you a considered opinion.

DECISIONS IN PRACTICE

Every decision involves an element of risk. If a client offers you way more work than you can handle, do you take it knowing that it means hiring in help? Or do you turn it down and risk losing future business from that client? When evaluating solutions – especially those with a financial outcome, the more closely you can test the outcome, the better your final decision will be.

1. IDENTIFYING THE ISSUE

You're about to be engaged in consultancy work for three clients on the following terms:

A.   20 hrs/wk for 6 months @ £25/hr
B.   10 hrs/wk for 6 months @ £29/hr
C.   8 hrs/wk for 6 months @ £19/hr

A and B are long-term, regular clients; C is a new connection with potential. The need for a decision is prompted by the arrival of client D, who makes you offers a lucrative deal with immediate effect:

D.   25 hrs/wk for 6 months @ £39/hr

> Do you accept client D's offer or
> do you turn it down?

2. IDENTIFYING THE ALTERNATIVES

> 1. Turn down client D's offer
> 2. Take on client D and work 63-hour weeks
> 3. Take on client D and let down other clients
> 4. Take on all four clients and hire in help

3. EVALUATE EACH OPTION

Now take a look at the implications of each of the four options.

> **OPTION 1: TURN DOWN CLIENT D**
>
> **+** Already engaged 38 hours a week,
> so no time available
> **−** Lose new client with enormous potential
> **−** Turn down lucrative rate of pay

> **OPTION 2: TAKE ON CLIENT D:**
> **WORK 63-HOUR WEEK**
>
> **+** Additional income of £25,350
> **+** Chance to impress a new client
> **−** Crippling schedule
> **−** May affect service to other clients
> **−** Disruption to family
> **−** I became self-employed so I could
> choose to work shorter hours

> **OPTION 3: TAKE ON CLIENT D:**
> **LET DOWN OTHER CLIENTS**
>
> **+** Alternative mix of clients could generate
> higher income for working less hours
> (*see Client Mix, right*)
> **−** No wish to let down existing client base
> (especially A and B)
> **−** Contracts signed with A, B and C – could
> risk legal implications by pulling out
> **−** Value personal reputation for reliability
> **−** Don't wish to be seen as a money-chaser

OPTION 4: TAKE ON CLIENT D:
HIRE IN HELP

+ Existing clients are kept happy
+ Now able to take on client D
+ As long as hired help can be brought in at less than £39/hour, the option is profitable
− Have to find and interview extra staff
− Managing staff takes time
− Left full-time employment because of dislike of managing staff

4. MAKE YOUR CHOICE

Only you can make the ultimate choice. The options, however, are all now laid out explicitly.

Option 1 would seem to be one to ignore straight away, unless, of course, you are satisfied with your existing client base, and happy with the money that they generate. The arrival of client D is appealing, but perhaps not enough to warrant the upheaval it would cause.

Option 2 would seem to be madness! And yet there are undoubtedly those for whom the idea of working over 60 hours a week for six months for an extra £25K would be acceptable.

Option 3 has a lot going against it. But do you really want to wreck a valuable relationship with your client? As you can see from the Client Mix box, there are ways of minimising the damage, but is it worth it for what might be a one-off job?

Option 4 seems to be the most appealing. But in some industries short-term hired help is like gold dust. Can you find someone in time? Will they be reliable? What will be your overhead in staff management? These questions will all play a part in your final choice.

5. IMPLEMENT YOUR DECISION

The systematic decision-making process should leave you in a position where you know what has to be done to put your option into practice. ●

EMOTIONAL DECISIONS

Decision making isn't always – and nor should it be – a purely logical matter. Experienced decision makers are often guided by intuitive thinking. Phrases like "my gut feel is …" or "I have a hunch that …" are commonplace in the most board rooms. Most satisfactory decisions, though, are those that can satisfy both the rational and intuitive sides of the brain. ●

CLIENT MIX

Option 3 has plenty of downsides. Letting down a client is one of *the* cardinal sins of self-employment. But by calculating the financial implications of different mixes of clients, you can at least weigh up the odds more effectively.

If you decide to set yourself a maximum working week of 45 hours, you have three mix options:

A+B+C £892/week for 38 hours.   Rate = £23.47/hr
A+D   £1424/week for 45 hours. Rate = £31.66/hr
B+C+D £1417/week for 43 hours. Rate = £32.95/hr

From these figures we can see that the optimum mix is probably B+C+D. It means that if you do go for option 3 you can benefit from the high hourly rate offered by client D, AND keep existing clients B and C happy – but client A still gets the elbow.

nuts
and bolts
maintenance

6

in this chapter...

keeping records

This next section is dull. VERY dull. But it's important. It deals with the thorny issue of book keeping. Since you only have to submit a tax return once a year, why do you need to do the books any more often than that? Surely an old shoe box containing a year's worth of sales and purchase invoices would do, wouldn't it? In your dreams.

LET'S FACE IT, unless you're an accountant you have to be pretty weird to get any pleasure out of book keeping. For most of us it's without question the single most tiresome aspect of being self-employed. But it's also an absolute necessity. There are two very important reasons why you need to keep good, accurate business records:

> **Without up-to-date books how can you hope to know the ongoing state of your business?**

- **To substantiate the state of you accounts for the purposes of legal committments – paying tax, in other words;**

- **To help you keep tabs on how your business is progressing.**

Just to fulfil your legal obligations it would clearly be possible to get away with a once-a-year burst of book-keeping activity (or four times a year if you are VAT registered). But without up-to-date books how can you tell how much free cash you have at your disposal? Or know when your invoices have been paid? Or how you are performing compared to your targets? You can only really guess. And that's not a sensible footing from which to operate even the simplest business.

YOU NEED A SYSTEM

Keeping your financial records up to date needn't be that complicated. For small businesses, or those that operate on the basis of a small number of transactions, it would be a waste of time creating a complex accounting process. A half a day with a spreadsheet program such as Microsoft Excel or Lotus 1-2-3 and you'll have a pretty nifty system in place. But even that's not a necessity – people kept records long before the advent computers. A couple of simple lined notebooks might well be adequate in some cases. Far more important is that you put together a methodical, consistent set of working practices.

DEALING WITH INVOICES

Invoices are the blood supply of any accounting system. An invoice represents either proof of a sale or proof of a purchase. One way or another, all of the figures in your books are derived from these invoices. Therefore it's critically important that in your business life you **NEVER EVER THROW AWAY AN INVOICE**.

The system you adopt for logging invoices in your accounts books will depend on the nature of your business and personal preference. Some will

THE SECRETS OF SELF-EMPLOYMENT #36
"Open three accounts – a business account, a tax account, and a personal account. don't put it all in the same pot. Mentally, you have to get into the habit of taking the taxes off first" – Alvin Hall interview in *Alodis* magazine.

prefer to keep their books permanently up-to-do date, logging sales and purchase invoices straight away; others will make updates on a periodic basis. If you choose the latter, try to get into good habits – do it regularly, the same time every week. Otherwise the likely consequence will be chaos or, worse still, lost paperwork. Not only will this waste valuable time but losing records of tax-deductible purchases can cost you "real" money. ●

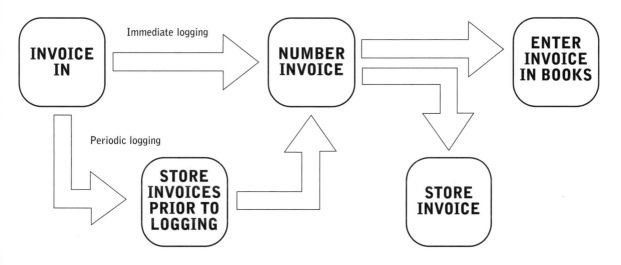

SALES AND PURCHASES

Many typical self-employed activities – especially those where services rather than products are provided – can survive happily with two sets of ledgers: one for sale and one for purchases.

ENTERING SALES

Every time you make a sale you must produce a numbered invoice or receipt for the client or customer. You should also retain a copy of this invoice for your own records. When you enter sales information into your sales book you don't need to include all of the detail, just the following:

- **Invoice date**
- **Invoice reference number**
- **Name of client or customer**
- **Value of the sale (including VAT).**

If you are registered for VAT, you also need to show the VAT paid and the value of the sale excluding VAT.

An additional column can be created to record invoice payments (along with the payment date, if you want to keep a record of how good your clients are at paying up). In the sample ledger below, ticks are shown to indicate payments.

LOGGING PURCHASES

The purchase ledger works in pretty much the same way. The main differences is that with sales invoices you are able to able allocate your own reference numbers; although purchase invoices

SALES (4th Quarter)					
Invoice	Date	Client	Gross	VAT	Net
√ 26	16-Feb	Sadlers	3254.75	484.75	2770.00
√ 27	19-Feb	Sadlers	3525.00	525.00	3000.00
√ 28	26-Feb	Sadlers	387.75	57.75	330.00
√ 29	4-Mar	Johnsons	587.50	87.50	500.00
√ 30	4-Mar	Johnsons	587.50	87.50	500.00
31	4-Mar	Fishers	822.50	122.50	700.00
√ 32	13-Mar	Johnsons	411.25	61.25	350.00
√ 33	13-Mar	Johnsons	387.75	87.75	330.00
34	22-Mar	Fishers	587.75	87.75	500.00
√ 35	27-Mar	Granada	387.75	87.75	330.00

Sales book: ticks represent those invoices that have been paid.

PURCHASES (4th Quarter)

Invoice	Date	Item	Gross	VAT	Net
√ 1	01-Mar-01	Mobile Phone – Orange	49.91	7.43	42.48
√ 2	12-Mar-01	Electricity - LEB	237.91	35.43	202.48
√ 3	16-Mar-01	Courier - SuperSpeed	7.40		7.40
√ 4	01-Apr-01	Mobile Phone – Orange	50.95	7.59	43.36
√ 5	01-Apr-01	Water – LW	170.01		170.01
√ 6	02-Apr-01	Phone Bill – BT	186.50	27.78	158.72
√ 7	03-Apr-01	Architect's Fees	3771.75	561.75	3210.00
√ 8	20-Apr-01	Stationery – Stallmont	122.29	18.21	104.08
√ 9	27-Apr-01	Reference Material – Smith&Gordon	4.75	0.71	4.04
√ 10	01-May-01	Mobile Phone – Orange	52.07	7.76	44.31
√ 11	02-May-01	Reference Material – Smith&Gordon	21.50	3.20	18.30
√ 12	04-May-01	Power supply	34.99	5.21	29.78
√ 13	05-May-01	Lighting (From France)	665.54	109.01	556.53
√ 14	13-May-01	Car Rental – Hertz	299.15	44.55	254.60
√ 15	13-May-01	Petrol	25.01		25.01

Purchase book.

● PURCHASE CATEGORY BREAKDOWN ●

Equipment	Maintenance	Consumables	Post/Phone	Travel	Office	Reference	Services
			42.48				
	202.48						
			7.40				
			43.36				
		170.01					
			158.72				
							3210.0
					104.08		
						4.04	
			44.31				
						18.30	
29.78							
					556.53		
				254.60			
		25.01					

Purchases by category. Each entry corresponds to an item in the purchase ledger

will usually contain the vendors own reference, as you enter each one you should allocate them sequential numbers. This should be written on the invoice and entered in the ledger.

You can also take each item from the purchase book and list it according to category. (The categories you choose will depend on the nature of your business.) In the example above, the first item in the purchase ledger is a mobile phone bill; that figure is entered under the category "post/phone" in the table above. It is an extension of the purchase ledger, and many book keepers show these categories as additional columns. Note that if you are VAT registered, the figures are shown EXCLUSIVE of VAT. ●

THE CASH BOOK

Many small businesses are based pretty well entirely on "cash". This means that irrespective of whether they are buying or selling, payment is made immediately. In these circumstances, the term "cash" covers ready money (notes and coins), cheques, direct debits, standing orders and credit card payments. The cash book is the most important ledger for businesses such as this – those that are small in scale but perhaps require frequent book keeping.

The cash book is the most important ledger for small businesses requiring an element of daily book keeping

All transactions are logged as either "cash" or "bank" items. If you look at the first entry in CASH BOOK (RECEIPTS) (*see below*) you can see that a customer named Joe Smith handed over a cheque for for £620.00. The specific details of the purchase can be found on an invoice that you've numbered 7254.

The CASH BOOK (PAYMENTS) at the foot of the page operates in a similar way: you can see that the opening transaction, for £721.87, was paid out to "Sadlers" using cheque 7562 from your business account.

CASH BOOK (RECEIPTS)

Date	Customer	Item	Bank	Cash
01-Mar-01	Joe Smith	Invoice 7254	620.00	
01-Mar-01	M. Houser	Invoice 7255	769.98	
01-Mar-01	M Marsden	Sale of car		2871.00
01-Mar-01	Inland Revenue	Rebate	1420.95	
01-Mar-01	M Gibbs	Invoice 7253	1670.01	
01-Mar-01	S Kowjciecz	Sale of lighting		85.00

Cash book for receipts

CASH BOOK (PAYMENTS)

Date	Supplier	Item	Bank	Cash
01-Mar-01	Sadlers	Cheque 7562	721.87	
01-Mar-01	Esso - Mill Green	Petrol		31.00
01-Mar-01	Orange	Direct debit	41.97	
01-Mar-01	Johnsons	Cheque 7563	1420.95	
01-Mar-01	Post Office	Special delivery		12.95
01-Mar-01	Fishers	Cheque 7563	85.00	

Cash book for payments: this could be extended to incorporate sales categories.

> **"** I spent £400 on a book-keeping program. Not being very technical I found it hard to set up, so I asked a neighbour, a certified accountant, if he'd take a look. I think he thought I was mad! He gave me a lined notebook and drew a dozen or so ruled columns on the first two pages. Sales were on the left; purchases on the right. He said that was all a set-up like mine needed right now. I was devastated! **"**
> **James Martens,** *caterer*

CHECKING YOUR BANK BALANCES

The great benefit of using this system is that at the end of a specified period it becomes possible to reconcile the balance in the cash books with both bank statements and cash receipts. On the bank statement for the first week of March, for example, both of the aforementioned payments will appear as individual transactions.

Although many people exhibit a glib attitude in this area, it's critical that, AT THE VERY LEAST, you get into the habit of crosschecking the balances in your cash book with those in your bank statement. If the totals do not match you can tell straight away that there is a problem: the bank may have entered a value wrongly, or cheques may have been lost or not yet cleared.

It's also strongly recommended that you do a transaction-level check every time a new bank statement arrives. ●

MORE COMPLEX REQUIREMENTS

If your business expands your record-keeping committments may increase dramatically. You may, for example, need a formal stock control system to keep track of incoming and outgoing goods – and cross-referencing that information with invoice payments.

Even more is required, though, if you become a formal employer. Indeed, at this point you effectively become a tax collector on behalf of the government. You will not only be responsible for calculating each of your employee's PAYE (Pay As You Earn) and National Insurace deductions, but also making those payments to the Inland Revenue. All of this makes you legally obliged to keep extremely detailed records relating to salaries and wages.

When you reach this point you will need a more sophisticated accounts set-up to cope with these new demands. There are plenty of software companies producing highly sophisticated off-the-shelf accounts packages equipped to deal with most small business needs. Until you reach that level, though, TRY TO KEEP THINGS AS SIMPLE AS POSSIBLE. ●

THE SECRETS OF SELF-EMPLOYMENT #37

You can pay your tax and VAT bills electronically – the Inland Revenue and Customs & Excise are even promising discounts; visit www.hmce.gov.uk and www.inlandrevenue.gov.uk

DO YOU NEED AN ACCOUNTANT?

If reading through the past few pages has neither taxed your brain nor sent you into a catatonic state, you might well be asking yourself why you should ever need the services of an accountant. After all, it's only adding up rows of numbers, isn't it? Don't be so hasty about this.

There's no doubt that most of us are capable of maintaining our books if the system is sufficiently simple. But you just might not want the hassle. Using the costly services of a qualified chartered accountant just for that purpose would be pretty excessive. There are plenty of cheaper personnel who can be hired to do that. The appeal of this is clear: you hand over a pile of purchase reciepts sales invoices, check stubs and bank statements

and what comes back is a completed set of books for the period. But there's a good deal more to accountancy than book keeping. Here are some other pretty good reasons why you might want to hire professional services:

● **To help get the business started**
● **To advice on whether to set up as a sole trader or limited company**
● **To advise on approaches to raising capital**
● **To nag you into doing your tax return**
● **To fill in your tax return**
● **To help set up cash-flow forecasts, profit-and-loss forecasts or your business plan**
● **To advise on VAT registration**
● **If your financial affairs are complex and require specialist knowledge**
● **To advise on the best start date for your tax year to suit your circumstances**
● **To ensure that you are maximising your personal allowances**
● **To give greater credibility to your tax return;**
● **To come with creative methods of reducing your tax bill**
● **To advise on pensions or other ways of creating tax-deductible expenses.**

If you are sole trader and are prepared to spend time researching the tax system, you may be able to cope with all of the above issues. But if you're serious about your business it's likely that you'll have more productive ways of spending your time. In short, decide how much you want to do and let an accountant take care of the rest. Things are different limited companies, however. You will need specialist advice here – not least for your legal obligations as a company director. ●

THE SECRETS OF SELF-EMPLOYMENT #38

"To cut your accountancy costs, have a bit of paper for each entry, which explains what the entry is about. This will be a big help if the Inland Revenue ever investigate your accounts" – Richard Murphy, article on www.alodis.com

CHOOSING AN ACCOUNTANT

There are over 10,000 accountants operating in the UK right now, so there are plenty from which you can choose. A good accountant will make your life easier, vanquishing the need for anxiety over such trifling matters as tax forms, legitimate business expenses and payment deadlines; make the wrong choice, though, and you could end up with a higher tax bill and, at the very worst, with a hefty fine. So how do you go about finding an accountant?

ASK AROUND

Don't bother to use Yellow Pages (or other similar directories). Ask family, friends, colleagues or (if you have a suitable relationship) competitors for personal recommendations. That obviously doesn't provides any sure-fire guarantee of quality, but it should point you in the right direction. Also, since cowboy reputations tend to get around quickly, you should hear about the ones to avoid.

CREDENTIALS

Unlike the medical profession, anyone can call themselves an accountant. So make sure that those you consider are qualified and registered with an appropriate body. These include: The Institute of Chartered Accountants (**www.icaew.co.uk** for England and Wales; **www.cca.org.uk** for Scotland) and the Chartered Association of Certified Accountants (**www.acca.co.uk**).

Of course, just because they are qualified (look for the letters ACA, FCA, ACCA or FCCA after their names) doesn't mean they'll necessarily be any better at the job, but at least they will be part of a regulated body.

WHAT SHOULD YOU PAY?

When you first engage an accountant you should always be clear what the scale of fees are likely to be, how they are calculated, and the precise service you can expect.

It's hard to give useful ball-park figures, since account fees reflect the amount of work that has gone into them. For a sole trader, a simple, well-kept set of records is likely to cost between £250-£400. Larger limited companies will pay considerably more because their accounts have to audited.

Your accountant's fee will also be higher if your books are in a poor state, or if you fail to supply infomration that has been requested.

VISIT IN PERSON

It's entirely possible to engage an accountant over the phone without ever having met face to face. This is not a good idea, though. By visiting them at their office you will get an immediate feel for whether a working relationship will be possible.

ASK LOTS OF QUESTIONS

Make sure you have a clear understanding of the way things will work. You need to know:

- **What information they want from you, and how long it will take them to deal with it**
- **When they need it**
- **What information they will send to you, and how often they'll send it**
- **Whether they will deal with all of your correspondence with the Inland Revenue**
- **If they will keep you informed of key dates in the tax year – such as tax return deadlines**
- **The scale of fees**
- **What those fees do and do not cover.**

understanding
taxation

Even if you engage a professional to calculate your taxes, you should have at least a rudimentary understanding of the way in which your deductions are calculated, and when you will be obliged to make payments.

"...In this world nothing is certain but death and taxes."

Benjamin Franklin (1706-1790)

IF YOU ARE self-employed, and your business is profiable, there are principally four different kinds of tax that you may have to pay:

- **Income Tax**
- **National Insurance**
- **Value Added Tax**
- **Corporation Tax**

We are all liable to pay income tax and national insurance; value added tax is only paid if you are VAT-registered; corporation tax only applies to those running limited companies. In some cases, capital gains tax (CGT) may also affect those disposing of plant, machinery and buildings.

INCOME TAX

The UK's approach to taxation was turned upside down a few years ago with the introduction of the self-assessment system. Under self-assessment you are responsible for the calculation of your own tax bill. The Inland Revenue will do this on your behalf, but it will be based on the figures you provide for them.

If you are self-employed you pay your taxes in three lumps. Two of them are "payments on account" – these are based on your tax bill for the previous year. The third is a "balancing payment" which accompanies your tax return, and so can be used to cover any outstanding payments (or hand back rebates if relevant).

The tax schedule should be firmly lodged in your brain.

- **JANUARY 31** **First payment on account**

- **JULY 31** **Second payment on account**

- **JANUARY 31** **Tax return**
  Balancing payment

YOUR TAX YEAR

The Inland Revenue has always traditionally worked to a year-end date somewhere during the month of April. This is known as the "fiscal year". Self-employed individuals and companies, however, can nominate their own year-end dates. From a calculation perspective, adopting the fiscal year makes life easier, but it's not necessarily the best thing to do.

If you nominate your own year-end early in the fiscal year – say, May or June – you will maximise the delay between earning your profits and paying tax. This helps cash flow when profits are on the increase. What's more it also provides you with a longer period in which to have your accounts drawn up. An alternative year-end also means that a proportion of your annual accounts will fall in a different fiscal year. Since these have to be worked out on a daily basis, the calculations will be a little more complex.

Whatever dates you choose, though, if you are registered for VAT MAKE SURE THAT IT COINCIDES WITH THE END OF A QUARTERLY VAT PERIOD. Take advice from your accountant on this issue.

"ALLOWABLE" BUSINESS EXPENSES

A legitimate business expense is an item that is used "wholly and exclusively" for business. Typically this includes:

- Costs of goods for sale
- Selling costs – advertising and promotion
- Your office – lighting, heating, cleaning, rent, telephones, printing, stationery, etc.
- Travel cost (not between home and work)
- Car hire
- Equipment leasing
- Staff costs
- Bank charges
- Business insurance
- Bad debts
- Legal costs.

There are many items with a somewhat ambiguous status – the rule here should be **if in doubt, claim it.**

TAXABLE PROFITS

Clearly the amount of tax you have to pay ultimately will be affected by your personal allowance and other individual circumstances. But what we're interested in looking at here is how we get to the final profitability figure – the amount on which your tax calculations will be based. To do this we take the profit figure from the accounts (essentially the difference between the balance from the sales ledger and the balance from the purchase ledger) and make adjustments for business expense elements that are not allowable for tax purposes.

THE SECRETS OF SELF-EMPLOYMENT #39

Don't sit on paperwork from the Inland Revenue. If you have an accountant, send it to him. If you deal with your own tax returns, don't leave it until until the last minute – if something goes wrong you won't have time to deal with it, and may end up with a fine.

DISALLOWED BUSINESS EXPENSES

These are the items that, although legitimate expenses in your purchase ledger, are not allowed to be included in your taxable profits. These costs must all be added back on to your profit figure:

- Costs/depreciation of capital equipment – buildings, vehicles, factory equipment
- Your own living expenses – including clothes and medicine
- Business entertainment expenses, such as meals or gifts of over £10.

CAPITAL ALLOWANCE

If you think that having no tax concessions on legitimate equipment sounds a little mean, don't worry: this is dealt with under what is called "capital allowances". These can be deducted from your profit figure – and are thus tax-deductible.

Over time, all equipment loses its value. The capital allowance you are allowed to claim is based on depreciation. This is a slightly complex area, since different types of equipment may have different rates of capital allowance. Here is a list of some of the more obvious items (for a full list take a look at the inland revenue's website at **www.inlandrevenue.co.uk**):

> 66 My previous accountant charged me £400 to do a set of unaudited books. I thought that was out of order, but needed them doing urgently, so I let him go ahead. Last year I decided to do the lot myself. I know my business isn't very complicated, but I managed to do the whole thing myself in about 2 hours. 99
> **Graeme Merson, *geologist***

> 66 I spent three or four evenings working out taxable profits for my first year in business. Six months later I discovered that I could have claimed capital allowance on equipment that I already owned before I started the business. How was I supposed to know that? I'll get an accountant next time. 99
> **Gary Boyle, *mobile studio engineer***

- Plant and machinery   40% 1st year
                                         25% thereafter
- Cars   25% (max. £3000)
- IT/communications   100%
- Industrial buildings   4% of original cost.

To put that into some sort of context, let's imagine that you have just bought a filing cabinet at a cost of £500. Your capital allowance for the first year would be 40% of £500 – £200. That £200 is then deducted from your profit figure. Thereafter, the filing cabinet has a value to your business of just £300. In the following year's accounts, your capital allowamce for the cabinet is 25% of £300 – £75; the cabinet is subsequently worth £225.

AND FINALLY...

So this is how we arrive at a taxable profit figure. There are other factors, but they would be unlikely to affect anyone taking responsibility for their own company accounts.

You may now be just starting to think that hiring an accountant may not have been such a bad idea after all. It's not that any of it is *terribly* difficult, it's just there is a great deal of legislative detail that you need to know. And regulations are changing all the time. ●

TAX FORM TIPS

- Make sure you have everything you need (there are supplementary pages to the standard 8-page from for the self-employed).

- The Inland Revenue will automatically send you a copy of your Tax return form in the post. If you lose it or throw it away you can download a new copy from the Inland Revenue website (**www.inlandrevenue.co.uk**).

- You can elect to return your forms electronically – the Inland Revenue is very keen to develop this approach, so look at their website for more details.

- A good technique for filling out important forms like your tax return is to make a photocopy and begin with that. You can make as many mistakes as you like before copying the correct information onto the real form.

- If you get stuck with your form, first take a look at the IR booklet *Self Assessment Your Guide.* Or else call your local tax for advice.

- Don't send any payment with your form! The Inland Revenue will demand it from you at the appropriate time – you needn't worry about that!

NATIONAL INSURANCE

There are four different categories of national insurance: Class 1; Class 2; Class 3; and Class 4. Class 1 contributions are paid by everyone in permanent employment. Class 2 and Class 4 contributions are only for the self-employed. For national insurance purposes, self-employed means sole traders or partnerships. Since directors of limited companies are technically employed by their companies, they pay Class 1 contributions. Class 3 contributions are voluntary.

CLASS 1

National insurance is one area where limited companies lose out. Both employee and employer are legally obliged to pay Class 1 contributions. This means that one-man limited companies pay twice: once for themselves, and once for their company. Payments are based on earnings. For 2001-2, employees pay 10% of their pre-tax weekly income between £66-£575; employers pay 11.9% on salaries above £87 per week.

CLASS 2

This is a calculated at a flat rate of £2 per week. All self-employed people are liable to this tax, although those with annual expected of earnings less than £3,825 can claim exemption. Class 2 contributions entitle you incapacity benefit, basic state retirement pension, maternity allowance and bereavement benefit.

CLASS 4

Self-employed workers with an annual income of more than £4,385 must pay Class 4 national insurance contributions. This is calculated at a rate of 7% on your taxable income, up to a maximum level of £29,900. ●

A sole trader with taxable profits of £27,500 would pay class Class 4 national insurance contributions of £1,786.05.

£27,500 - £4,385 = £23,115

7% of £23,115 = £1,786.05

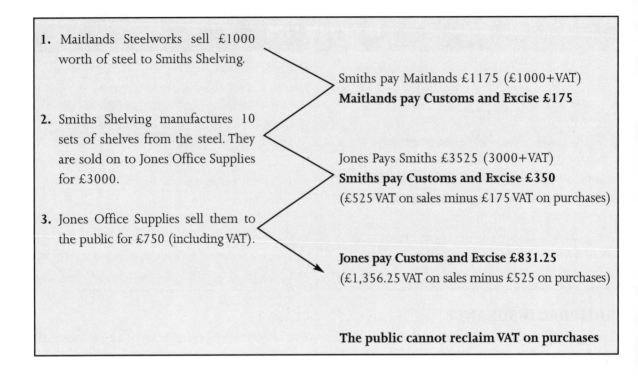

1. Maitlands Steelworks sell £1000 worth of steel to Smiths Shelving.

Smiths pay Maitlands £1175 (£1000+VAT)
Maitlands pay Customs and Excise £175

2. Smiths Shelving manufactures 10 sets of shelves from the steel. They are sold on to Jones Office Supplies for £3000.

Jones Pays Smiths £3525 (3000+VAT)
Smiths pay Customs and Excise £350
(£525 VAT on sales minus £175 VAT on purchases)

3. Jones Office Supplies sell them to the public for £750 (including VAT).

Jones pay Customs and Excise £831.25
(£1,356.25 VAT on sales minus £525 on purchases)

The public cannot reclaim VAT on purchases

VALUE ADDED TAX

As consumers, we are forced to pay Value Added Tax on most items that we buy. VAT is an "indirect" tax – it's only paid when the purchase is made. Businesses that are registered for VAT must charge VAT for their products or services, but are allowed to reclaim the VAT element of the purchases they have made. The difference is paid to the government's Customs and Excise department, making every VAT-registered business responsible for collecting taxes. The standard rate of VAT is currently 17.5%.

To see how this all works, let's look at the example in the box above. As you can see, it's quite a simple (if long-winded) process. Each of the businesses may in turn charge VAT on sales and reclaim VAT on purchases. The chain only comes to an end with the eventual customer, who is unable to reclaim VAT.

REGISTRATION RULES

If your sales are greater than £52,000 a year, then it's compulsory that you register for VAT. All goods and services are grouped within one of the following categories:

- **Exempt – no VAT is paid**
- **Zero-rated (0%) – books, food, drink, children's clothes, exports**
- **Standard-rated (17.5%) – goods and services**
- **Reduced-rated (5%) – domestic fuel**

Note that exempt is not the same as zero-rated. Neither one charges VAT on what they sell (exempt items are not taxed; zero-rated items are taxed, but at 0%). The exempt category, however, cannot reclaim VAT paid on purchases; the zero-rated can. This means that costs for the exempt category will be 17.5% higher.

It is possible to voluntarily register, even if your sales are well below the legal threshold. This makes sense only when you are selling products or services to VAT-registered businesses: it doesn't matter to them that your charge is 17.5% higher – they'll simply reclaim it from Customs and Excise. The advantage in this situation is that your costs will be 17.5% lower than if you had not been registered.

VAT RETURNS

Payments to (or rebates from) Customs and Excise are normally made on a quarterly basis. The VAT return is a single sheet in which you have to declare your sales and purchases for the period, VAT on sales and purchases, details of sales and purchases made outside of the UK, and your final

VAT INSPECTION

Don't mess with the VAT man. He has considerable powers at his disposal. If you make late payments or major accounting errors in your return you may face a hefty fine.

Periodically, a VAT inspector will pay you a visit. This can be a bit scary, but as long as your books are in order and give a truthful account of your business you should have no worries.

quarterly balance. You make a payment for that amount and enclose a cheque with the form. There is also an option of making your VAT returns electronically.

If your annual turnover is less than £300,000 you can elect to switch to annual accounting. This offers a benefit in cashflow and less necessary paperwork. But you do need to discipline yourself if you are to avoid the nasty shock of a big bill at the end of the year. ●

CORPORATION TAX

If you are operating as a limited company you will pay standard income tax as an employee of your own company. This will be based on the salary you draw from your business. On top of that, however, you also must pay corporation tax on your company's taxable profits. There are two different rates of corporation tax – the "full rate" and the "small-company rate". Since the British government's definition of what constitutes a small company is one whose taxable profits does not exceed £300,000, we won't worry too much about the full rate.

Companies with taxable profits up to £10,000 pay corporation tax at a starting rate of 10%. The top rate of 20% applies to companies with taxable profits of £50,000-£300,000. For those between £10,000 and £50,000, there are marginal rates of between 10% and 20%.

Directors of limited companies are also able to pay themselves dividends and fringe benefits. Working out an appropriate way of paying the least amount of taxes but gaining maximum benefits is a skill that for most of us would be best left to an accountant. ●

legal advice

Whether we are accepting a proposal from a client, taking a lease on new premises, negotiating a price for our products, or chasing late payments, each one is subject to the intricacies of our legal system. Whilst we can deal with most of these matters using our own judgement, sometimes we may need to seek the views of a professional.

LIKE AN ACCOUNTANT, there are numerous everyday tasks for which a legal professional – usually a solictor – could be engaged. Most of the time, though, we're not going to want to do that. It simply wouldn't be financially viable, for example, to pay a hefty solicitor's fee to draw up an employment contract every time you needed a few days freelance help: in practice, a clear, unambiguous letter on headed notepaper that details dates of employment, rates of pay and a work brief would usually be quite satisfactory. Similarly, every time a new client gave you a contract to sign, you *could* first pay your solicitor to check it out in detail. But you don't.

In spite of the possible legal implications, most of the everyday transactions we have to face are not terribly complicated, and can be handled with a bit of care and common sense. That's not to say that there aren't some very useful functions that the legal profession can perform on our behalf.

BUSINESS ADVICE

Solicitors come in many shapes and forms, each with their own specialties. A solicitor should be able to:

● **Advise on setting up your business**
● **Provide template contracts**
● **Advise on the complexities of employment law (don't even think about becoming an employer without consulting a solictor)**
● **Advise on property leasing**
● **Assist with debt recovery**
● **Use expertise to help raise capital**
● **Brief you on product protection, such as patenting or registering a trademark**
● **Advise on personal guarantees for loans.**

CHOOSING A SOLICITOR

Many of the same conditions apply for finding a good accountant (*see page 147*), so ask around for recommendations. Since law is such a wide-ranging

THE SECRETS OF SELF-EMPLOYMENT #40

Never let yourself be pressured into signing a contract before you're ready. If you need time to think it over, take it: be highly suspicious of any party that demands an immediate response.

DEBT RECOVERY

We've already touched on the subject of chasing late payments on page 113. As we said there, bringing in the law should be a last resort. If you're a service provider, the small claims court is the best solution to chasing payments from a tight-fisted client. But unless you're very unlucky that sort of thing should not happen very often.

If, however, you operate in a business where you deal with a larger number of small customers, bad debt is likely to be a more common problem. Since the amounts involved may well be too small to bother the small claims court a debt-collecting agency may be the best solution.

Agency fees are based on a percentage of the money they manage to recover, so clearly it's in their interest to take any action they deem necessary to get results. This usually starts with an explicit letter pointing out that failure to pay will result in their details being passed on to a credit-reporting company. The fear of a damaged credit rating is often enough to secure immediate payment.

Of course, this won't work for everyone. There will come a point a point where you have to decide whether legal action is appropriate, or, if it simply isn't worth the hassle, then to write off the debt.

subject, not every solicitor you approach will be equally well-placed to give the same expert advice. That said, since solicitors usually operate from within a practice, there ought to be a range of skills available among the various partners. But you need to check.

Costing legal advice is more problematic than estimating accountant costs, but be suspicious of anyone who can't give you at least a ballpark figure. At the very least you should be given a daily rate.

FREE ADVICE

Lawyers For Your Business is a scheme run by the Law Society, and backed by, among others, the Federation Of Small Businesses. The aim is to put growing owner-managed businesses together with solicitors (it's claimed that only one in ten small businesses ever consult a solicitor).

Solicitors taking part in the scheme offer a free initial consultation followed by a clear assessment of future costs. But if you don't want or need such advice just now, it's certainly worth getting hold of the step-by-step free guides that use flowcharts to tackle a wide variety of legal problems, and then set out the implications of the possible answers.

You can find out further information and details of participants from the Lawyers For Your Business website (**www.lfyb.lawsociety.org.uk**). Or you can telephone 020 7316 5521 for your copy of the guides. ●

personal finance

Being self-employed does have some downsides. Besides there being no paid holiday, we also lose out on company pension perks. And when we want to buy property we have to convince lenders that we are not forever on the brink of bankruptcy. But with careful planning and thought, these needn't be insurmountable difficulties.

HOWEVER DISTANT THE prospect may seem to us right now, there will come a point when our working days are no more. Retirement should be a time for comfort and taking things easy, but if we fail to make sensible provisions during our working lives, it's more likely that we'll end up having to count out pennies to make ends meet.

Without income from an occupational pension or a private plan, you'll be forced to rely on a state pension. Since the current single person's pension is £67.50 (boosted to £78.45 under the Minimum Income Guarantee), unless you live a very frugal lifestyle, you are likely to experience an extremely severe fall in your standard of living. And this will be a common fate: according to the Federation of Small Businessess, more than 50%

More than 50% of Britain's self-employed have made no pension provisions for their retirement

of Britain's self-employed have made no provision at all for retirement.

PENSION PLANS

For sole traders or self-employed operaters working within a partnership, there is little choice other than making their own arrangements by saving with a pension provider, such as an insurance company. The pension provider uses experience and expertise to invest monthly payments in a cash fund. At a future set date the money can used to provide either a regular income or a tax-free lump sum (or a combination of both).

If you are self-employed with no significant inheritances in the pipeline, or capital assets that can be disposed of on retirement, the message is simple: **YOU MUST GET A PENSION PLAN**.

Governments past and present have been keen for us to make our own provisions for retirement. Consequently there are generous tax incentives for taking out private pension plans. You can, for example, deduct pension payments from your taxable income. There are, however, limits to the amount you can invest as a sole trader and still claim this benefits. These depend on your age and your net profits (ranging from 17.5% of net profits for the under-35s, to 40% for over the 60s).

COMPANY MATTERS

If you are operating as a limited company there is a vastly improved range of options for creating your own pension scheme. As well as taking out a private pension plan you can also set up your own

STAKEHOLDER PENSIONS

You've doubtless heard a good deal about these. They were introduced by the government in April 2001 as an alternative to occupational or private pension plans in an effort to encourage saving among the 25% of the population who have no such provisions. The target is the middle-income earner on salaries of between £10-18,000 a year.

Stakeholder pensions are intended to be low-cost, affordable and easy to set-up (you can even do it over the phone). They also must fulfill certain legal criteria, irrespective of which company is selling the product. Most of the traditional pension providers can set up a stakeholder pension.

company fund. This allows you to channel very large sums, minimising your tax bill. This approach is especially advisable for those starting a fund late in life. If you have a very large income at your disposal you should seek advice from an independent financial advisor on this one. ●

SELLING ON RETIREMENT

For most "knowledge-based" self-employed people, the business revolves entirely around their skills. As a result, when they retire their business retires with them. In more traditional areas, however, the owner may have the choice of selling off a business as a going concern. Many self-employed people think of this as being their old-age pension. This is risky course of action. What happens if your retirement coincides with a downturn in business? Or if ill health forces you to retire earlier than you had planned? Furthermore, if on retirement you sell, give away or dispose of your business you may be liable to pay capital gains tax.

This approach may yield an impressive result, but is not advisable as an alternative to a conventional pension plan.

THE SECRETS OF SELF-EMPLOYMENT #41

Use the Internet to work out your retirement income with online calculators. Try http://moneycentral.com.msn.co.uk /pensions

MORGAGE LENDERS

Until very recently getting a mortgage was a major deal if you were self-employed. Lenders wouldn't even talk to you if you couldn't supply them with three years worth of audited accounts. If you passed that hurdle you then had to face the fact that maximum amount loaned would be much smaller than your "permie" counterpart. He could expect to be offered three times his salary; the best you could hope for would be three times your net profits.

As anyone who has ever been self-employed will attest, the net profit figure rarely gives a true reflection of income. This is because that figure is the result of your revenue after

> **With white-collar job security increasingly rare, the self-employed are no longer seen as such a risk.**

legitimate business costs have been subtracted. Equally, directors of limited companies who pay themselves artifically low salaries to avoid income tax, are penalised in the same way. It seems that in the eyes of mortgage lenders, the self-employed have traditionally been viewed as second-class borrowers.

SELF-CERTIFICATION

The good news, though, is that some changes are afoot. With self-employment edging towards 15% of the total workforce, it's clear that a potentially lucrative market has not been satisfactorily served. With the job security that many mortgage lenders traditionally valued so much about the permanent white-collar job market now increasingly rare, the self-employed are no longer seen as such a risk. And – guess what? – they now seem to be falling over themselves for our business.

The most significant change to have taken place is in the basis for what we are realistically allowed to call our income. This has come about through a system known as SELF-CERTIFICATION. The loan applicant makes a simple declaration of what he or she sees as a realistic assessement of income – in practice this will clearly fall somewhere between your total revenue (maximum) and net profits (minimum). The borrower doesn't have to provide proof, but most lenders who operate under this system (which still isn't all mortgage companies) insist that an accountant be employed to assess the viability of the business.

> ❝ I have nearly 25 years of successful self-employed experience... but I get so angry at the treatment meted out by mortgage lenders... I feel like I'm an "undesirable" whenever I walk into one of their offices. The worst time was about 10 years ago. I'd just separated from my husband and was looking for a flat. The problem was that we'd lived off his huge income – I drew only a tiny salary from my company, and had deliberately cut back on work the previous two years when my daughter was born. Consequently, the offers I got were risible. In the end, I was forced to take a permanent job I didn't want *just* so I could get a decent mortgage. As soon as my first mortgage payment went through I resigned and revived my company! I hope things are easier nowadays. ❞
> **Jan Warbeck,** *public relations executive*

MORTGAGE TYPES

All of this is a quite a big step forward for the self-employed. After as little as six months in business it may be possible to get an 80-85% mortgage based on a self-certified income level. The interest rate will usually be slightly higher than most standard high-street mortgages, but not enough for you to feel ripped off.

Mortgages come in a variety of different forms. These days, however, following the disasterous demise of the interest-only "endowment" policy, the "repayment" mortgage remains the most popular. This works on a simple premise that you pay back a monthly figure, based on the prevailing interest rate, for the full life of the mortgage.

A development that has only taken off in the UK in recent years is the so-called "flexible" mortgage system. This type of policy has a number of benefits that should be of particular interest to the self-employed. The main difference is that it doesn't rely exclusively on fixed monthly payments, but allows more to be paid off when business is brisk, or "payment holidays" when cash is short.

After only six months in business it may be possible to get an 85% mortgage

THE SECRETS OF SELF-EMPLOYMENT #42
If in doubt, use a broker. If you get quotes from the average high-street lender and they reject you, this will count against your credit score

SHOP AROUND

Forty years ago there was relatively little choice when it came to finding a mortgage. Things are very different now. We have realistic access to any product offerred by any company operating anywhere in the country – or even further afield. The complexity and choice of products on the market has resulted in the emergence of a new mortgage broking industry. A good independent broker will have an in-depth knowledge of the products on the market. Such people are worth tracking down. The brokerage fee may put up the initial costs of your mortgage, but it could save you a great deal of money in the future. ●

WEB CONTACTS

The following websites contain relevant information to mortgages for the self-employed:

www.mortgage-next.com
www.money.guardian.com
www.mortgages.sterling.co.uk
www.nationwide.co.uk
www.on-linemortgages.co.uk
www.non-status-mortgage.co.uk
www.mortgagebrokersuk.com
www.yourmortgage.co.uk
www.1st-mortgage-brokers.co.uk

where
next?

7

in this chapter...

the network effect

It's not *what* you know, but *who* you know. That is the very essence of networking. We live in tribal times. Nowadays, though, school, university and social class are less likely to bond us to our fellow tribesmen than lifestyle and personal interests. In the 21st century it's all about making connections with like-minded souls.

TO SAY THAT networking is essential when you are self-employed is a giant understatement. Whatever it is you do for a living – whatever product or service you produce or sell – you are tapping into an interlinked group of interested parties. As these networks expand your business activities reach a wider potential audience. Networks are important for many reasons:

● **Support for people in the same boat**
● **Spreading word of your business activities**
● **Broadening your client or customer base**
● **Cross-pollination of business skills and technical know-how.**

HOW ARE NETWORKS BUILT?

Even if you have just one client and live an almost hermit-like existence, you have a network – all be ita very small one. Networks happen as a direct result of business and social activity. But they need nurturing and feeding, or else the links wither and die.

BUSINESS NETWORKS

Networking goes on naturally in all workplaces – at the coffee machine, in the canteen, in the corridors… but if you are self-employed you have to work hard to build your own.

Fundamental to any network is that each part can bring something useful or desirable to the others in the "loop". So the whole thing begins with your business ethos. Always aim to impress. If you strive to perform your work brilliantly, reliably, in an amenable manner, (and in a way that your client *knows* that you've done the job well – a little well-placed crowing never does any harm!), those with whom you work, or have

> **❝** I'd advise caution when recommending contacts for employment. A client was in a fix. I hadn't the time to step in so I suggested they call someone from my network of contacts. She'd always been reliable when she'd worked for me, but her time with my client was evidently one disaster after the next. They terminated her contract after only a month. Since then she's been too embarrassed to speak to me. But I later found out that my name was mud around their boardroom as a result. I've lost a good contact and seriously damaged a client relationship just by trying to help out. **❞**
> **Claire Colvin,** *publishing consultant*

worked, will automatically begin contributing to your network on your behalf. Quality work is usually rewarded with repeat business. Each new commision will bring you contact with different personnel to impress. As *they* move on to new employers they take your reputation with them – that's more of an endoresement than any CV or mailshot could ever be.

It's critically important, however, that you maintain contact with those you've worked with – you'll only stay fresh in their minds if YOU make the effort to stay in touch. make a point of seeing them from time to time over a drink or a meal. Make sure that they are on your mail-shot list. If you're worried about appearing to be hustling for business, a card with your professional details (and a small gift if appropriate) at Christmas should still be an effective memory jogger.

To meet a broader range of people engaged in your industry, join a professional organisation, such as a trade association, guild or institute, and attend their functions. Here you will come into

contact with people in your field who might be able to offer you support, advice, feedback on industry-wide developments and, above all, contacts. Similarly, track down the websites of like-minded professionals. Training courses can can also prove fertile territory to meet people and build confidence, while improving your skills.

SOCIAL NETWORKS

Self-employment can be a lonely business. If you work in an office you have the choice of going out at lunchtime with friends; if you work alone, you don't have the same opportunity. Therefore creating network of people in the same boat can be a real lifeline. To build a network, find a few self-employed people in your area and suggest meeting up for lunch. The rule is simple: every new member has to bring a self-employed friend to the next meting. Soon there will be a diverse group of people with one thing in common – their working lifestyle. ●

THE SECRETS OF SELF-EMPLOYMENT #43

Here's the first rule of networking: NEVER LEAVE HOME WITHOUT YOUR BUSINESS CARDS. (And even if you don't leave home, keep them close at hand – you never know who might pop in.)

extra hands

Although most of the subjects we've covered so far apply to all small businesses, we've generally used the term "self-employed" to mean soloists, owner/managed operations, one-man bands. But some of us have never really quite got to grips with the idea that there are only 24 hours in a day. Sometimes we need a little help.

IT'S NOT THAT DIFFICULT to "accidentally" take on more work than we can manage. It happens to us all from time to time. If we're to avoid the slippery slop of working ludicrous hours, it means hiring in extra help or subcontracting out some of the work.

PERMANENT EMPLOYEES?

Think VERY carefully before taking the decision to become a full-time employer. If you do this you take on ENORMOUS legal obligations. Maximum working hours, paid holiday and paid sick leave are but a few of an employee's statutory rights. Furthermore, you have to pay national insurance contributions and are responsible for calculating and deducting income tax under the PAYE system.

The following Inland Revenue booklets tell you exactly what your responsibilities are in this area: *Thinking Of Taking Someone On?* (CWL3); *Employer's Guide To PAYE* (CWG1)

The safest approach is to go for short-term freelance assistance. How successfully you can do this depends on the nature of the job market for your industry. There are some, such as publishing, where freelancing is almost as commonplace as permanent employment, so finding temporary staff may not be a major problem. In areas where there are skill shortages, though, you may expect to pay correspondingly high rates, and have trouble enticing suitable candidates.

An employer's legal obligations to temporary freelance staff are by no means clear-cut. As long as both parties have agreed the work to be done, period of employment and the rate of pay, in theory there should be no problems. (And despite Sam Goldwyn's legendary quip about a verbal contract not being worth the paper it's written on, a spoken agreement *is* binding – no matter how unwise that that might be.)

If you engage the same person to work on your premises for greater than a year, the Inland Revenue – should they find out – may well argue that this person is a full-time employee of yours. Both you and your subcontractor should watch out for this.

In many cases, finding appropriate assistance will be down to personal networks. It's always a smart idea to get to know good, reliable people working in your own sphere. Passing work around can also help to create useful reciprocal relationships: sometimes your assistant may have too much on at times when you are quiet.

If you can't find help in this way then you are left with two other possibilities: advertising or employment agency. The former can be a rather hit-and-miss business, and you have to pay for the advert whatever the result. Agencies will send

THE SECRETS OF SELF-EMPLOYMENT #44
The work involved in taking on staff shouldn't be underestimated. As well as time spent recruiting and interviewing, when your new staff starts working you'll have to make time to manage them. Sometimes it might just be better to the turn the work down.

prospective staff for interview. If you take them on you pay the agency directly. Both of these courses of action would suggest a longer-term commitment was needed. ●

SELECTING STAFF

However informal an arrangement you intend to make with your sub-contractor, the most sensible starting point is with a job description. This ensures that all the way through, from advertising the vacancy (if appropriate) to actually doing the work, both you and the other party know unequivocally what is expected of one another. For most freelance purposes this won't need to be a particularly lengthy document:

- **Job title**
- **Overall responsibilities of the job**
- **Specific tasks and activities**
- **Rate of pay/hours of work.**

Unless you know the candidate and his or her work personally, you should always ask for a current CV. This in itself should be the first "weeding out" stage. Compare the candidates' achievements with the requirements of your job description. If it fits the bill, arrange to meet and interview them.

Staff interviewing is a skilled business art, and not one that many owner/managers possess. Your task will be primarily to decide whether the candidate is capable of doing the job. But there are plenty of other factors that come into play: do they have an agreeable personality? Do you actually *want* to work with them. ➔

THE INTERVIEW

Here are some very basic tips to help you with your interviews. Some of them might cause seizures among professionals who teach this sort of thing, but we're more interested in being practical here.

To begin with, keep things in perspective. This isn't a corporate affair. You're not looking for someone who wants you to provide them with a career development path, so don't waste time querying the bogus leisure pursuits on their CVs. You've got a very specific job for them to do; if you're confident they can do it, and you think that working with them will make for a mutually beneficial experience, then what more could you ask for?

- **Don't be hasty. It's easy to form faulty impressions very quickly**
- **Don't be put off by superficial matters like hairstyle, accent or style of clothes**
- **Try to establish a rapport. See if you are likely to get on in a working environment**
- **The only probing questions you need bother with should be related to the job you have on offer**
- **Be on the alert for signs of evasiveness when discussing specifics of the work (typical signs are lack of eye-contact, fidgeting and avoiding straight answers)**
- **The candidate should do most of the talking, apart from when questioning you**
- **Don't use closed questions – the ones that can be answered with a yes or no**
- **Look out for any interesting skills that the candidate might be able to pass on to you.**

> **❝** I left my job in Chicago because I didn't enjoy managing people. I wanted to get back to basics. I worked alone very successfully for about a year. Then during the course of one week, two clients asked me if I could handle entire projects for them. They were real plums, so I agreed and started looking for reliable help. That was five years ago. I still work in my same tiny office, but now I head up a "virtual" team which sometimes pushes towards 20. Some of them are based thousands of miles away – several are even in England. It's fun trying to arrange team meetings. We tried all sorts of things, including using an empty Internet chat room! **❞**
> **Erik Petite, *MC books***

Once you've made an offer and had it accepted, draw up a very simple contract of engagement. This need be little more than the job description you wrote at the start of the process – or it may also contain clauses relating to copyright or other issues that may be relevant. Make two copies and ensure that you both sign and date each one. Each of you keeps a copy. Anything less than this simple written contract leaves potential for misunderstanding. In practice, you'll find that many client/sub-contractor relationships have nothing firmer than a telephone conversation to back them up. Nonetheless, it's always better to have things written down. ●

MANAGING STAFF

Taking on a freelancer may only be the start of your concerns. Next there is the issue of day-to-day management to worry about. If you don't want the hassle of worrying about productivity value for money it's much more sensible to agree a fee for the entire job. This also makes financial planning a good deal more straighforward. If that's not acceptable, give a clear indication of exactly how long you expect the job to take. (The formula here is **days allowed = the flat fee you had in mind ÷ daily rate**.)

How you manage your freelancer will largely depend on the practical issue of location. If you generally work alone then it's unlikely that you'll have room for additional bodies. Your freelancer may, of course, insist on working in his or her own home/office. In this case, you'll have to exercise "remote" management. The ability to run a "virtual" team will become one of the widely sought-after business arts of the 21st century (*see left*).

> ## The ability to run a "virtual" team will become one of the business arts of the 21st century

THE BRIEF
Get things off on the right foot by ensuring that you communicate a coherent brief to the person doing the work. This is SO FUNDAMENTAL, and yet so often overlooked. Both manager and staff are always happier when they both know what to expect. A good brief should contain a set of measurable tasks or goals with a clear schedule for when it has to completed.

PROGRESS REPORTING
If you are managing staff remotely, make sure that you hold periodic face-to-face meetings. Try to hold them regularly at the same time. This enables you to monitor progress both from quantitative and qualititative points of view. Keep your meetings brief and to-the-point, though. Don't forget

that you are effectively paying for the time you spend in conference.

If you are not happy with some aspect of the work done so far don't be aggressively critical. First check that the brief has been understood, or that you have stated it clearly. If the situation fails to improve, make your dissatisfaction known in a calm and professional manner. Reiterate the quality and quantity of the work you expect. Terminating the contract should be an absolute last resort.

DO UNTO OTHERS...
A final message: you know how much you HATE IT when clients don't pay your invoices on time? (Which is nearly always.) When *you* become the client, do your bit to redress this balance. Be a good egg: **PAY UP PROMPTLY**. ●

THE SECRETS OF SELF-EMPLOYMENT #45
Once you've discovered a good, reliable person to whom you can sub-contract your overflow with complete confidence, hang onto them. Treat them like gold dust. A network of such people will make those decisions whether to take on extra work that much easier.

topping up on skills

Education and training have always been the traditional routes to career enhancement, but lavishing time and money on courses can seem like a luxury for many busy self-employed workers. This can be short-sighted. Without continual development of existing skills, you risk losing your edge in the marketplace – something that no competitor in any field can afford to do.

WHEN YOU'RE BUSY doing your own thing, it's easy to ignore happenings in the outside world. For many self-employed operators, without the regular input from peers and managers, and without the workplace training opportunities open to most employees, there's always a danger of being removed from developments going on in your industry. You can't let this happen. You have to take responsibility for continually training and educating yourself.

You have a responsibility to train and educate yourself continually

So how do you identify your own needs? This a tough question. How, do you know, for example, that you'll soon need to be familiar with a new piece of computer software when you don't even know that it exists yet? The answer is in MARKET INTELLIGENCE. You don't have the luxury of being spoon-fed this kind of information by your "superiors", so you need to keep yourself in the loop. Fellow freelancers, trade magazines, newsletters, society meetings and, of course, the Internet are all crucial sources of the latest industry information.

> ❝ Self-employment is about constantly reinventing yourself. You have to keep moving forward in terms of what you can offer, the markets you are in, or your channels to market. That puts constant demands on you to develop new knowledge, ideas and skills. ❞
> **Calvert Markham, *management consultant***

> **“** I like to take the opportunity to "move in" with my clients from time to time. Although nearly all of my work is done at home, I occasionally get the opportunity to work in-house for a month or so. This has so many benefits. Firstly it allows me to bond with the client on a personal level, and get to know about upcoming projects before some of my competitors. More important, however, is that I get a feel for changes in my industry, new approaches to working, new developments in technology. It's important research – and I get paid at the same time. **”**
>
> **Ashley Kinnear, *network specialist***

THE SECRETS OF SELF-EMPLOYMENT #46

When you work for yourself it's not always easy to stay abreast of market trends. This is where networking is so important to the self-employed. Talk constantly to those in your field – pick up the vibe on new directions and skills that need adding to your portfolio.

NETWORKING

The quality of your networking will make all the difference. Most self-employed workers come into contact with a far wider array of professionals within their industry than they ever could working with one company. There is no better opportunity than this to make important long-lasting connections. This is also where those with greater confidence and social skills can score heavily – a ten-minute chat over a pint with the Business Development Director can yield more useful information than a day spent scouring websites and trade journals.

A ten-minute chat over a pint may yield more information than a day scouring websites and trade journals

ENVIRONMENT

Workplace learning is perhaps the most valuable of all. It provides a context in which theory becomes practice. But when you generally work in isolation from your clients – either at home or in your own office – you can easily lose track of the subtle shifts in working practice that inevitably take place in any industry. Try to keep up to speed with new developments in your clients' workplace environments. Make sure that you pay them regular visits. And remember, as much as it may go against the grain for some self-employed workers, the occasional in-house work stint can also turn into a valuable reconnaissance exercise. ●

TAX BREAKS

If you can take out the time for formal training courses, you should plan for these costs when creating budgets. If you can show that it is beneficial to your business, all education and training costs are legitimate business expenses.

TRAINING COURSES

How do you know when you need additional training? That's easy — there's *always* something useful that you can learn. If you believe otherwise you will become a dinosaur.

If your market knowledge indicates that there are new technical skills you require, then you have no choice but to go out and get them. Time your training carefully, though. It's not much use working through a course if you won't be putting your new skills into action for another year. The most effective educational experiences are always those where formal study can immediately be consolidated with practical experience.

In terms of upgrading your day to day working practices, you need to exercise a little common sense and realism. Make a list of aspects of your business that cause you difficulties or anxiety. Are you constantly struggling to hit deadlines? A time management course might be a solution. Do you get nervous or

> ## THE SECRETS OF SELF-EMPLOYMENT #47
> Training and education is largely wasted if you can't put the things you have learnt quickly into practice. Try to organise courses so that they fall between projects, otherwise there is a danger of your being too busy to implement change when you return to your work.

tongue-tied when you approach potential clients? Personal communications training might do the trick. Do you think of yourself as being a lousy salesperson? You'll find plenty of useful courses from which you can choose.

EVALUATING A COURSE

As many professional trainers will attest, there are rarely large numbers of self-employed workers attending their courses. The reason for this is simple: most of them are too busy out there "doing the business". There is an opportunity cost to attending a formal training course, and that's the amount of income you lose while sitting in the lecture theatre. Can you be certain the benefits to potential business will outweigh the costs to your business? That's the question every one of needs to ask. Unfortunately the answer is not usually easy to evaluate, which

> **It's not much use doing a course if you won't be putting newly acquired skills into action for another year**

FINANCING TRAINING

You can apply for a career development loan, which will lend you from £300 to £8,000 to cover up to 80% of the course fees and legitimate costs (including books, equipment and childminding). Repayment can be deferred for up to two years.

is presumably why some of us seem so reluctant to commit to such action.

Finding the right course can also be problem. The training industry has more than its fair share of cowboy operators, so the best way to choose is always by personal recommendation. If the course is offering specialised training then look for the endorsement of an appropriate professional body. Before you start any course, always obtain a detailed description of its content. You can never assess the worth of a course just from its title.

WHAT FORM?

Training comes in many different guises. The type you choose will depend largely on the time and money you plan to invest, and the modes of learning to which you are best suited:

- **Do-It-Yourself** Studying an appropriate book is a legitimate form of training. Useful and inspirational tips can also be acquired from training videos and CDs. The advantages are that it's cheap, and you choose the study times, which you can fit around your work. The downside is that it requires discipline, and there is on nobody on hand to point out errors or misinterpretation of material.

- **Long-term, full-time study** At the other end of the scale, you could take time out to go into full-time education. Realistically, there are few well-established self-employed workers who could afford (or would even want) to do this. Although post-graduate degrees such as MBAs have definite currency, this approach is most likely to be used by those wanting to shift the slant of the business (or even move into a completely unrelated area). You should assume that once you've completed your course you'll have to find a new client base.

- **Part-time study** This is good compromise for some. Most universities and colleges now offer some form of part-time or distance study. This usually requires a commitment of two or three evenings a week, and will take at least twice as long to complete as a full-time course. It requires considerable dedication, though – and drop-out rates are high.

- **Short full-time study** Courses lasting just one or two days are often more satisfactory in that they generally aim to provide in-depth coverage of a limited amount of material. This enables you to focus on your training needs more specifically. ●

ONLINE TUITION

A major growth trend in the US (which means it's soon bound to catch on over here), is for learning via "online universities". This approach offers useful advantages to the self-employed: it's cheap; it can be done at your desk; and you can work on the course at any time you choose.

Courses are usually run in short modules and are "teach-yourself" in nature, although there is normally a course tutor who goes online at specific times to answer queries. Although this can't ever replace one-to-one personal tuition, it does have other advantages. By taking a course run from the US – where most major trends in business theory and software begin – your course content may be more up-to-date.

end of
the road?

Self-employment is not for everybody. Some people operate more effectively within a structured corporate family. Others just miss the hustle and bustle of the office – there's no way you can really replicate that by working on your own. And some businesses simply don't survive. Whatever your circumstances, though, you should be able take something positive away from your experience, something that serves you well in the next phase of your working life.

RUNNING YOUR OWN business is one of the most fulfilling of career pursuits, but it can also be extremely tough going. There is no question that a signifiant body of those who try it for themselves return to the conventional market at some point in the future. Of that group, the vast majority abandon self-employment primarily because their businesses are not performing well (or have already gone under).

For some, being surrounded by others is fundamental to their personal happiness

> **❝** I miss the interaction and activity of having a "real" job. I'd like to go back, but I currently earn double the salary I would be able to get in full-time employment. That's too big a cut to take. **❞**
> **Jenny Eddington, *book packager***

There is a smaller group, however, for whom it's just not their thing. There seem to be two main reasons for wanting to return to full-time employment. Some people just can't get to grips with the periods of isolation – being around others is fundamental to their personal happiness. The other main factor that seems to win back a lot of people is a need to be a part of a hierarchy, with personal goals set using the promotion system as a benchmark. If you're self-employed you have to set those for yourself.

Of course, there's is no right or wrong way. As always, the best advice is for us to do what is most likely to make us happy. ●

IN TOO DEEP?

If you've put into practice the lessons taught in this book, you are less likely to fail than most small businesses. But sometimes, things just don't work out. It may even have nothing at all to do with the way you manage your business. Perhaps a genuine demand for your product or service just isn't there; maybe you can't produce and sell competitively enough; maybe outside factors such as market conditions or the global economy are working against you.

THE WRITING'S ON THE WALL

It can be devastating for an entrepreneur to accept that the business he or she has created has run aground. Like a great relationship gone sour, it can be painfully difficult to let go. So at what point do you hold your hands up and say "enough is enough"?

Here are some of the warning signs that indicate that a business in jeopardy:

- **When existing customers start leaving in increasing numbers**
- **You start sellling off assets to pay debts**
- **When you hit (or exceed) your bank's overdraft limit**
- **When you are unable to raise any further capital**
- **When you only pay your outstanding bills when threatened with legal action**
- **When your liabilities (what you owe) are greater than your assets (what you own)**

> **"** I could've lost everything in the recession of the early 90s. My biggest client, a property developer, got into severe difficulties when the market collapsed. He committed suicide owing me £200,000. He owed millions to various creditors, so small fry like me were well down the pecking order. I didn't get penny. I had to remortgage the family house to pay off my own debts. I didn't go under, but it's taken me 10 years to get back to where I was in 1991. **"**
> **Paul Reeves, *building contractor***

Dealing with a crisis situation like this calls for whole new approach. It requires you to be calm, and realistic in your assessment of the situation. The worst thing that can happen is panic.

Now you need to take professional advice, either from your accountant, financial advisor, or a Business Link advisor. As impartial observers they may be able to see rational solutions that you are too involved to notice. They will almost certainly know if it's time to quit. ●

THE SECRETS OF SELF-EMPLOYMENT #48

When you are used to dealing with every detailed aspect of your business, it can be easy for a megalomanic mindset to develop. Never be too proud to accept advice, especially where the future of your business is at stake.

YOU DON'T HAVE TO BE BANKRUPT

A large number of sole traders and owner-managed limited companies work as freelance or contract service providers. Only a tiny proportion of these return to the permanent job market having been declared insolvent.

If you're a sole trader, terminating your company can be a simple matter. All you really have to do is stop trading. Whenever you return to permanent employment you resume paying taxes on the PAYE system. In theory this automatically alters your tax status (although in practice, if your new employer hasn't got his act together, you may find yourself having to contact your local tax office to prevent being taxed at source at an emergency rate).

You will also need to complete a final set of accounts for your company, so that your taxable income for that year can be added to your tax return. (If your books show that you were running at a loss, it can legitimately be deducted from the tax you've paid via PAYE.) At this point, the Inland Revenue will need to know the precise date that you ceased trading so that national insurance contributions can be recalculated.

The situation for limited companies is a little more messy, and best left to an accountant to sort out.

If you are VAT registered, you will need to inform Customs and Excise of your plans. They will expect you to complete a final VAT return. If you haven't received a visit from a VAT inspector in recent years, you might find that sprung on you at this time as well.

Don't forget that you may also get clobbered for capital gains tax on any assets remaining in your business. In practice, this is unlikely to be an issue unless you have buildings or a lot of undisposed plant and equipment. If this does happen, makes sure your assets are assessed at their correct "deducted" value (*see page 148*).

PULLING THE PLUG

Once the business has reached a point where the money you owe (your liabilities) exceeds the value of your assets (everything you own), you are "insolvent". At worst, this could mean bankruptcy for a sole trader, or liquidation for a limited company or partnership. Both of these have legal ramifications for your future, so let's look at some ways to avoid such a fate.

VOLUNTARY OPTIONS

Most of us have run into finanical difficulties at some time. When this happens you need to be realistic and accept your circumstances. This is not the time to bury your head in the sand. It could be that you are solvent, but are not a in a position to pay off your debts: you may have plenty of assets tied up the way of plant and equipment but no cash. The aim here is to avoid one or more creditors taking bankruptcy procedings against you. **You only need to be £750 in debt for this to happen**. Here are some possible courses of action:

● **Informal Arrangements** Begin by discussing the matter with your creditors. This may take guts, but is a necessary step. Try to hammer out an informal arrangement by which you can pay off your debt according to an agreed schedule. This is the cheapest solution, but it still leaves you open to bankruptcy procedings if the creditor changes his mind.

● **Administration Order** If you have less than £5,000 owing and there is a county court judgement for at least one of your debts you can apply for a court administration order. If accepted (which means supplying evidence that you will be able to cover the debt at some stage) a repayment schedule is agreed. You then make payments directly to the court, which are distributed to your creditors, who can no longer file for your bankruptcy.

- **Other Options** There are further complex possibilities, but these largely require the use of a professional insolvency practicioner.

BANKRUPTCY AND LIQUIDATION

For sums above £750, a creditor can choose to open bankruptcy proceedings. This will begin with a formal demand for payment arrangements to be made. If you fail to comply with the request within 21 days, your creditor can file a bankruptcy petition in a bankruptcy court. If this accepted, from that moment all of your personal assets (including your home) are controlled by a trustee (a licensed insolvency practicioner or the Official Receiver) who will sell them to put towards your debt repayment. You remain a bankrupt for three years (two if you volunteer bankruptcy). Following that period, any further debt from your bankruptcy is written off.

THE SECRETS OF SELF-EMPLOYMENT #49

We live in a culture that has little sympathy for failure, even if many successful entrepreneurs have lost businesses (or close shaves) behind them. The inventor Edison would have had no truck with that: "I have not failed. I've just found 10,000 ways that won't work." Don't get too disheartened.

Limited companies that become insolvent are "liquidated". The assets are seized and used to pay off the debt. The company is then disolved. Because of the nature of a limited company, its directors are not usually personally liable for corporate debts.

You can find useful information on this subject from **www.insolvency.co.uk**, the website of the government's Insolvency Service. ●

GOING BACK TO THE JOB MARKET?

Whatever your reasons for returning to the world of permanent employment, you should be able to use the experience to boost your credentials. Even if you didn't quite achieve what you set out to do, make a virtue out of new skills you've had to acquire. You will have become a more rounded person as a consequence of running your own business. You will have become: more productive; more organised; a better communicator; more confident; used to thinking on your feet; a multi-tasker; adept at thinking your way around problems. You will have practical experience of finance, taxation and company law. You may even have new-found experience of the recruitment and management of staff. All of these are very positive assets by any standards, so why be modest about them?

contacts

**THE SECRETS OF
SELF-EMPLOYMENT
#50**

IF YOU THERE'S
SOMETHING YOU CAN'T DO,
FIND SOMEBODY WHO
CAN HELP.

GOVERNMENT SITES

www.businesslink.co.uk

www.enterprisezone.org.uk

www.britishchambers.org.uk

www.btgplc.com

www.bvca.co.uk

www.companies-house.gov.uk

www.dti.gov.uk

www.inlandrevenue.gov.uk/home.htm

www.hmce.gov.uk

DIRECTORY SITES

KOMPASS UK	www.kompass.co.uk
KELLYS	www.kellys.co.uk
BRAD	www.brad.co.uk
Business Pages	www.businesspages.co.uk
Thomson Local Directory	
	www.thomweb.co.uk

ACAS READER LTD
PO Box 16
Earl Shilton
Leicester
LE98ZZ
Tel: 01455-852225
Fax 01455-852219

ACCORD CORPORATE SERVICES
50 Vauxhall Bridge Road
London
SW1V 2RS
Tel: 020-7834 6666
Fax 020-7931 07000

ADVERTISING STANDARDS AUTHORITY (ASA)
2 Torrington Place
London
WC1E 7HW
Tel: 020-7580 5555
Fax 020-7631 3051

ADVISORY CONCILIATION AND ARBITRATION SERVICE (ACAS)
Brandon House
180 Borough High Street
London
SE1 1LW
Tel: 020-7210 3000
Fax 020-7210 3645
www.acas.org.uk

AROMATHERAPY ORGANISATIONS COUNCIL
PO Box 19834
London SE25 6WF
Tel: 020-8251 7912

ASSOCIATION OF BRITISH CHAMBERS OF COMMERCE
4 Westwood House
Westwood Business park
Coventry
CV4 8HS
Tel: 024-7669-4484
www.britishchambers.org.uk

ASSOCIATION OF CONSULTING ACTUARIES (ACA)
1 Wardrobe Place
London
EC4V 5AH
Tel: 020-72483163
Fax 020-7236 1889
www.aca.org.uk

BOOKSELLERS ASSOCIATION OF GREAT BRITAIN AND IRELAND
Minister House
272 Vauxhall Bridge Road
London
SW1V 1BA
Tel: 020-7834 5477
Fax 020-7834 8812
www.booksellers.org.uk

BREWERS AND LICENSED RETAILERS ASSOCIATION (BLRA)
42 Portman Square
London
W1H 0BB
Tel: 020-7486 4831
Fax 020-7935 3991Web
www.blra.co.uk

ACUPUNCTURE COUNCIL
Park House
206-208 Latimer Road
London
W10 6RE
Tel: 020-8964 0222
Email:info@acupuncture.org.uk

BRITISH BANKERS, ASSOCIATION
Pinners Hall
105-108 Old
Broad Street
London
EC2N 1EX
Tel: 020-7216 8801
www.bba.org.uk

BRITISH CHAMBER OF COMMERCE (BCC)
4 Westwood House
Westwood Business Park
Coventry
CV4 2HS
Tel: 01203-694492
Fax01203-694690/695844
www.britishchambers.org.uk

**BRITISH EXPORTERS ASSOCIATION
(BExA)**
Broadway House
Tothill Street
London
SW1H 9NQ
Tel: 020-7248 3163
Fax 020-7236 1889
www.bexa.co.uk

**BRITISH FRANCHISE ASSOCIATION
(BFA)**
Thames View
Newton Road
Henley-On-Thames
RG9 1HG
Tel: 01491-578049
Fax: 01491-573517
www.british-franchise.org.uk

**BRITISH INSURERS AND
INVESTMENT BROKERS
ASSOCIATION (BIIBA)**
BIIBA House
14 Bevis Marks
London
EC3A 7NT
Tel: 020-7623 9043
fax: 020-7626 9676
www.biiba.org.uk

**BRITISH INTERNATIONAL FREIGHT
ASSOCIATION (BIFA)**
Redfern House
Brodwells Lane
Feltham
TW13 7EP
Tel: 020-8844 2266
Fax: 020-8890 5546
www.bifa.org

**BRITISH LIBRARY SCIENCE
REFERENCE AND INFORMATION
SERVICE**
Science 1 Reading Room
British Library
96 Euston Road
London
NW1 2DB
Tel:020-7412 7454/7977
Fax: 020-7412 7453

**BRITISH VENTURE CAPITAL
ASSOCIATION (BVCA)**
Essex House
12-13 Essex Street
London
WC2R 3AA
Tel: 020-7240 3846
Fax: 020-72403849
www.bvca.co.uk

BUSINESS CONNECT (WALES)
Tel: 0345-969798

BUSINESS LINK (ENGLAND)
Tel: 0345-567765

BUSINESS SHOP (SCOTLAND)
Tel: 0800 787878

**CENTRE FOR ACCESSIBLE
ENVIRONMENTS**
Nutmeg House
60 Gainsford Street
London
SE1 2NY
Tel: 020-7357 8182
Fax: 020-7357 8183
www.cae.org.uk

**CHARTERED INSTITUTE OF
PATENT AGENTS**
Staple Inn Buildings
High Holborn
London
WC1V 7PZ
Tel: 020-7405 9450
Fax: 020-7430 0471
www.cipa.org.uk/cipa

**CHARTERED INSTITUTE
OF TAXATION**
12 Upper Belgrave Street
London
SW1X 8BB
Tel: 020-7235 9381
Fax: 020-7235 2562
www.tax.org.uk

CHARTERED INSURANCE INSTITUTE
20 Aldermanbury
London EC2V 7HY
Tel: 020-7606 3835

COMMISSION FOR RACIAL EQUALITY
Elliot House
10-12 Allington Street
London
SW1A 5EH
Tel: 020-7828 7022
Fax: 020-7630 7605
www.cre.gov.uk

COMMITTEE OF SCOTTISH CLEARING BANKERS
Drumsheugh House
38Drumsheugh Gardens
Edinburgh
EH3 7SW
Tel:0131-299 1326

COMPANIES HOUSE (ENGLAND AND WALES)
Crown Way
Cardiff
CF4 3UZ
Tel: 01222-388588
Fax: 01222-380900Web
www.companieshouse.gov.uk

COMPANIES HOUSE (SCOTLAND)
37 Castel Terrace
Edinburgh
EH1 2EB
Tel 0131-535 5800
Fax: 0131-535 5820
www.companieshouse.gov.uk

COMPANIES REGISTRY (NORTHERN IRELAND)
IDB HOUSE
64 Chichester Street
Belfast BT1 4JX
Tel: 01232-234488
Fax:01232-544888

COMPETITION ACT ENQUIRY LINE
Tel: 020-7211 8989

CONSUMER CREDIT TRADES ASSOCIATION (CCTA)
Tennyson House
159-163 Great Portland Street
London
W1N 5FD
Tel: 020-7636 7564
Fax: 020-7323 0096

COUNTRYSIDE AGENCY
John Dower House
Crescent Place
Cheltenham
Gloucestershire
GL50 3RA
Tel: 01242 521381
Fax: 01242 584270
www.countryside.gov.uk

DEPT OF THE ENVIRONMENT, TRANSPORT AND THE REGIONS
Eland House
Bressenden Place
London
SW1E 5DU
Tel: 020-7 890 3333
www.detr.gov.ukDirect

MARKETING ASSOCIATION (UK)
Haymarket House
1 Oxendon Street
London
SW1Y 4EE
Tel: 020-7321 2525
Fax: 020-7321 0191
www.dma.org.uk

DISCRIMINATION ACT HELPLINE
Tel: 0345-622633
www.disability.gov.uk

DTI BUSINESS IN EUROPE HOTLINE
Tel: 020-7215 8885
Fax:020-7215 8884

DTI CONSUMER AFFAIRS DIRECTORATE
Department Of Trade And Industry
1 Victoria Street
London
SW1H 0ET
Tel: 020-7215 5000
Fax: 020-72222629
www.dti.gov.uk

DTI CONSUMER SAFETY PUBLICATIONS
Admail 528
London
SW1W 8YT
Tel: 0870-150 2500
Fax 0870-150 2333

DTI COUNTRY DESKS
Tel: 020-7215 5000

DTI EXPORT EXPLORER
Tel: 020-7215 8885
www.dti.gov.uk/ots

DTI EXPORT PUBLICATIONS
Tel: 0870-150 2500
Fax: 020-7215 2482

DTI PUBLICATIONS ORDERLINE
Tel: 0870-150 2500

OWNERSHIP SCOTLAND (EOS)
Building 1 Templeton
Business Centre
Templeton Street
Bridgeton
Glasgow
G40 1DA
Tel: 0141-554 3797
Fax: 0141-5545163

EMPLOYERS' HELPLINE
Tel: 0345 143143
Tel: 0845 6070143

ENGLISH PARTNERSHIPS
16-18 Old
Queen Street
London
SW1H 9HP
Tel: 020-7976 7070
Fax: 020-7976 7740
www.englishpartnerships.co.uk

EQUAL OPPORTUNITIES
Commission
Overseas House
Quay Street
Manchester
M3 3HN
Tel: 0161-833 9244
Fax: 0161-835 1657
www.eoc.org.uk

EURO PREPARATIONS UNIT
Tel: 08456 010199
www.euro.gov.uk

EXPORT MARKET INFORMATION CENTRE (EMIC)
British Trade International
Kingsgate House
66-74 Victoria Street
London
SW1E 6SW
Tel: 020-7215 5444

FEDERATION OF RECRUITMENT AND EMPLOYMENT SERVICES LTD
36-38 Mortimer Street
London
W1N 7RB
Tel: 020-7323 4300
Fax: 020-7255 2878
www.fres.co.uk

FEDERATION OF SMALL BUSINESSES
32 Orchard Road
Lytham St Anne's
FY8 1NY
Tel: 01253-720911
Fax: 01253-7146651
www.fsb.org.uk

FINANCE & LEASING ASSOCIATION
Imperial House
15-19 Kingsway
London
WC2B 6UN
Tel: 020-7836 6511
Fax: 020-7420 9600
www.fla.org.uk

FINANCIAL SERVICES AUTHORITY
25 The North Colonnade
Canary Wharf
London
E14 5HS
Tel: 020-7676 1000
Fax: 020-7676 1099
www.fsa.gov.uk

HEALTH AND SAFETY EXECUTIVE
Information Line
Tel: 05415-45500

HOME OFFICE EMPLOYERS'
HELPLINE
Tel: 020-8649 7878

HSE BOOKS
PO Box 1999
Sudbury
CO10 6FS
Tel: 01787-881165
Fax: 01787-313995
www.open.gov.uk

IFA Promotion
17-19 Emery Road
Brislington
Bristol
BS4 5PF
Tel: 0107-9711177

INDUSTRIAL COMMON OWNERSHIP
FINANCE LTD (ICOF)
115 Hamstead Road
Handsworth
Birmingham
B20 2BT
Tel: 0121-523 6886
Fax: 0121-554 7117
www.icof.co.uk

INDUSTRIAL COMMON OWNERSHIP
MOVEMENT (ICOM)
Vassalli House
20 Central Road
Leeds
LS1 6DE
Tel: 0113-246 1737

INDUSTRIAL SOCIETY
Robert Hyde House
48 Bryanston Square
London W1H 7LN
Tel: 020-7262 2401
Fax: 020-7479 2222
www.indusoc.co.uk

INFORMATION SOCIETY INITIATIVE
(ISI) INFORMATION LINE
Tel: 0345-152000

INSOLVENCY SERVICE PUBLICATIONS
Alcove marketing Group
PO Box 100
Swadlincote
DE12 7DR
Tel: 01530-272515

INSTITUTE OF CHARTERED
ACCOUNTANTS IN ENGLAND
AND WALES
PO Box 433
Moorgate Place
London
EC2P 2BJ
Tel: 020-7920 8100
Fax: 020-7920 0547
www.icaew.co.uk

INSTITUTE OF CHARTERED
ACCOUNTANTS OF SCOTLAND
27 Queen Street
Edinburgh
EH2 1LA
Tel: 0131-225 5673
Fax: 0131-2253813
www.icas.org.uk

INSTITUTE FOR COMPLEMENTARY
MEDICINE
PO Box 194
London
SE16 1QZ
Tel: 020-7237 5165

INSTITUTE FOR EMPLOYMENT
CONSULTANTS (IEC)
3rd Floor Steward House
16A Commercial Way
Woking
GU21 1ET
Tel: 01483 766442
Fax: 01483-714979
www.iec.org.uk

INSTITUTE OF EXPORT
Export House
64 Clifton House
London
EC2A 4HB
Tel: 020-7247 9812
Fax: 020-7377 5343
www.export.org.uk

INSTITUTE OF PRACTITIONERS IN ADVERTISING (IPA)
44 Belgravia Square
London
SW1X 8QS
Tel: 020-7245 7020
Fax: 020-7245 9904
www.ipa.co.uk

INSURANCE BROKERS REGISTRATION COUNCIL
Higham Business Centre
Midland Road
Higham Ferrers
Northants
NN10 8DW
Tel: 01933 359083

INTERACTIVE MEDIA IN RETAIL GROUP (IMRG)
5 Dryden Street
London
WC2E 9NW
Tel: 07000-464674
www.imrg.org

INTERNATIONAL CHAMBER OF COMMERCE
ICC United Kingdom
14-15 Belgravia Square
London
SW1X 8PS
Tel: 020-7823 2811
Fax: 020-7235 5447
www.iccwbo.org

LAWYERS FOR YOUR BUSINESS
Freepost
PO Box 61
London NW1 0YP
Tel: 020-7405 9075
Fax: 020-7691 2007

LENTA (LONDON ENTERPRISE AGENCY)
4 Snow Hill
London
EC1A 2BS
Tel: 020-7236 3000
Fax: 020-7329 0226
www.lenta.co.uk

ENTERPRISE DEVELOPMENT UNIT
LEDU House
Upper Galwally
Belfast
BT8 6TB
Tel: 01232-491031
Freephone: 0800-0925529
Fax: 01232-691432

MAILING PREFERENCE SERVICE
Haymarket House
1 Oxendon Street
London
SW1Y 4EE
Tel: 020-7766 4410
Fax: 020-7976 1886
www.dma.org.uk

MONEY MANAGEMENT REGISTER
Tel:0117-9769444

NATIONAL ASSOCIATION OF MUTUAL GUARANTEE SOCIETIES
ScrivenHouse
Richmond Road
Bowdon
Altrincham
Cheshire
WA14 2TT
Tel: 01625 521231
Fax: 01625-521269
www.namgs.com

NATIONAL BUSINESS ANGELS NETWORK (NBAN)
Third Floor
40-42 Cannon Street
London
EC4N 6JJ
Tel: 020-7329 2929
Fax: 020-7329 2626
www.nationalbusangels.co.uk

NATIONAL FEDERATION OF ENTERPRISE AGENCIES
Trinity Gardens
9-11 Bromham Road
Bedford
MK40 2UQ
Tel: 0161-242 2200
Fax: 0161-242 2400
www.ncc.co.uk

NATIONAL COMPUTING CENTRE
Oxford House
Oxford Road
Manchester
M1 7ED
Tel: 0161-242 2200
Fax: 0161-242 2400
www.ncc.co.uk

NATIONAL MINIMUM WAGE ENQUIRIES
Freepost PHQ1
Newcastle-Upon-Tyne
NE98 1ZH
Tel: 0845-6000 678
Fax: 0845-845 0360
www.dti.gov.uk/ir/nmw

NATIONAL NEWSPAPERS, MAIL ORDER PROTECTION SCHEME
16 Tooks Court
London
EC4A 1LB
Tel: 020-7269 0520
fax: 020-7404 0106
www.mops.org.uk

NCM CREDIT INSURANCE
3 Harbour Drive
Capital Waterside
Cardiff
CF1 6TZ
Tel: 01222-824000
Fax: 01222-824003
www.ncmgroup.com

NORTHERN IRELAND BANKERS'
Association
Stokes House
17-25 College Square
EastBelfast
BT1 6DE
Tel: 01232-327551

OFFICE FOR HARMONISATION IN THE INTERNAL MARKET (TRADE MARKS AND DESIGNS)
Avenida De Aguilera 2003080
Alicante
Spain
Tel: 003496-513 9100
Fax: 003496-5139173
ww.oami.eu.int

OFFICE FOR NATIONAL STATISTICS PRESS AND INFORMATION DIVISION
Government Building
Cardiff Road
Newport
NP9 1XG
Tel: 01633-812973
Fax:01633-812599
www.ons.gov.uk

OFFICE FOR THE DATA PROTECTION REGISTRAR
Wycliffe House
Water Lane
Wilmslow
SK9 5AF
Tel: 01625-545745
Fax: 01625-524510
www.dpr.gov.uk

OFFICE OF FAIR TRADING
15-25 Bream's Buildings
London
EC4A 1PR
Tel: 020-7211 8000
Fax: 020-7211 8800
www.oft.gov.uk

OFFICE OF FAIR TRADING PUBLICATIONS
PO Box 36
Hayes UB3 1XB
Tel: 0870-6060321
Fax: 0870-6070321
www.oft.gov.uk

PATENT OFFICE
(inluding Patent Office Search And Advisory Service)
Concept House
Cardiff Road
Newport
NP9 1RH
Tel: 0645-500505
Fax: 01633-814444
www.patent.gov.uk

PERIODICAL PUBLISHERS ASSOCIATION
Queen's House
28 Kingsway
London
WC2B 6JR
Tel: 020-7404 4166
Fax: 020-7404 4167
www.ppa.co.uk

THE PRINCE'S TRUST
18 Park Square East
London
NW14LH
Tel: 020-7543 1234
Fax: 020-7543 1200
www.princes-trust.org.uk

REDUNDANCY PAYMENTS SERVICE
Tel: 0500-848489

REGIONAL SELECTIVE ASSISTANCE DIRECTORATE
1 Victoria Street
London
SW1H 0ET
Tel: 020-7215 2565
Fax: 020-7215 2562

REGISTRY OF CREDIT UNIONS AND INDUSTRIAL AND PROVIDENT SOCIETIES
IDB House
464 Chichester Street
Belfast
BT1 4JX
Tel: 01232-234488

REGISTRY OF FRIENDLY SOCIETIES (ENGLAND AND WALES)
25 The North
Colonnade
Canary Wharf
London
E14 5HS
Tel: 020-7676 1000
Fax: 020-76761099

REGISTRY OF FRIENDLY SOCIETIES (SCOTLAND)
58 Frederick Street
Edinburgh
EH2 1NB
Tel: 0131-226 3224

THE RETAIL DIRECTORY
Newman Books
32 Vauxhall Bridge Road
London
SW1V 2SS
Tel: 020-7973 6402

ROYAL INSTITUTE OF PUBLIC HEALTH AND HYGIENE
28 Portland Place
London
W1N 4DE
Tel: 020-7636 1208
www.riph.org.uk

ROYAL MAIL SALES CENTRE
35 Rathbone Place
London
W1P 1HQ
Tel: 0345-950950
Fax: 020-7239 2092
www.royalmail.co.uk

SCOTTISH TRADE INTERNATIONAL
120 Bothwell Street
Glasgow
G2 7JP
Tel: 0141-2282808

SITPRO (SIMPLER TRADES PROCEDURES BOARD)
Tel: 020-7215 0800 (helpdesk)

SOCIETY OF PENSION CONSULTANTS
St Bartholomew House
92 Fleet Street
London
EC4Y 1DH

TECHNICAL HELP TO EXPORTERS
British Standards Institution
Information Centre
389 Chiswick High Road
London
W4 4AL
Tel: 020-8996 7111
Fax: 020-8996 7048
www.bsi.org.uk

TELEPHONE AND FAX PREFERENCE SERVICES
Haymarket House
1 Oxendon Street
London
SW1Y 4EE
Tel: 01932 414161

THOMSON DIRECTORIES
Customer Care Department
296 Farnborough Road
Farnborough
GU14 7NU
Tel: 01252-555555
Fax: 01252-378051
www.thomweb.co.uk

**TRADE INTERNATIONAL
(NORTHERN IRELAND)**
Industrial Development Board
For Northern Ireland
64 Chichester Street
Belfast
BT1 4JX
Tel: 01232-233233

TRADE UK
The Dialog Corporation PLC
The Communications Building
Leicester Square
London
WC2H 7DB
Tel: 020-7925 7808
Fax: 020-7925 7770
www.tradeuk.com

WELSH OFFICE
Cathays Park
Cardiff
CF1 3NQ
Tel: 01222-825097

WORKRIGHT INFORMATION LINE
Tel: 0845-6000925 (for leaflet)

index

acknowledgements

The author would like to thank: Michele Hirst at Carlton and Andrew Erskine at Alodis/Mongrel for their time and effort in getting this project put together in the first place; Carla Lally at Alodis/Mongrel for her extensive comments on each chapter – they may not always have been that gratefully received, but they've helped to shape this into a better book; Alvin Hall for a groovy and inspiring foreword; all the folks who completed my case-study questionnaire, and who passed them onto friends of friends of friends all over the world; SJ and JSJ for entertainment; Irwin for producing *Songs In The Key Of Z* – the sountrack to this project (in my mind, at least); and, of course, to the beautiful Junoir ("You are my inspiration, Junoir, Junoir/The perfect combination, Junoir").

Finally, I'd just like to mention my late father, Ronald Burrows, whose dogged determination to spend his entire working life with one company has probably been the single most important inspiration to my own career – cheers, Dad.

Support
as you go

Alodis is the only organisation in the UK that exists solely to support self-employed professionals. Membership is free and open to anyone who is a self-employed professional or thinking of becoming one. Currently our members come from a wide variety of professions – from aromatherapists to accountants, and marketing consultants to surveyors.

As well as offering services, Alodis is campaigning for better recognition of the needs of the self-employed community by the Government and other institutions, such as banks. Our campaigns focus on the issues that directly affect your working life, such as late payment, simplification of tax, and faster access to capital. Alodis is also using the buying power of this previously under-represented group to obtain special deals in areas such as telecommunications, finance and travel for its members. Alodis services currently include:

ALODIS MAGAZINE
The only monthly publication for self-employed professionals, with practical business advice, information and inspiration. Available on subscription only, it has helped many readers save money and work more efficiently. Call the number at the bottom of this page to take out your subscription.

ALODIS WEBSITE
www.alodis.com – offers advice and information on a huge variety of areas, including business planning, tax and VAT, networking, marketing yourself, obtaining grants. Plus discounts and special deals from Alodis partners.

ALODIS ASSISTANT
The unique PA service run by real PAs. It can answer calls, take messages, and book meetings on your behalf. It synchs up with your computer and PDA, so you can stay in touch when you're on the move or provide cover when you are on a trip or holiday.

ALODIS FINANCE MANAGER
The first ever software package specially tailored for the needs of self-employed professionals. Includes video advice on book-keeping, expenses, VAT, dealing with red tape, as well as the latest easy-to-use financial management software, Quicken Deluxe 2001

For free membership, or to find out more details about Alodis services, ring: 0800 038 4888.
Alodis.[Insert logo] Now working for yourself doesn't mean by yourself